Chronicles of a Believer

Christ in you
the Hope of Glory

Chronicles of a Believer

Don McCain

Chronicles of a Believer

Cover design by David Warren
Author photo and cover photo by Benjamin McCain

Published by WordCrafts Press
Tullahoma, TN 37388
www.wordcrafts.net

Contents

Forward

Donnie was my young community evangelist who helped me establish Uptown Baptist Church in 1976. His enthusiasm for Christ and his charismatic story-telling abilities drew young and old alike into a relationship with Christ. In fact, he is known as *the story man*.

The stories in this book are true-life stories that will encourage you to exercise your faith in Christ to experience your own great adventures and victories. Donnie's stories remind me of those early years of miraculous events we enjoyed together.

That is what young believers do - they come to Christ as children of faith believing that God can do anything. These God-events prove that Donnie's God *is* God. Stay expectant in your faith and see what great things God has for you.

Rev. James Queen
Founder of Uptown Baptist Church
Retired Executive Director
of Chicago Metropolitan Baptist Association

I will open my mouth and tell stories. I will speak about things that were hidden. They happened a long time ago. We won't hide them from our children. We will tell them to those who live after us. We will tell them about what the LORD has done that is worthy of praise. We will talk about his power and the wonderful things he has done.

Psalm 78:2 & 4

Preface

First John 1:1-4, *"That which was from the beginning, which we have heard, which we have seen with our eyes, which we have looked upon and our hands have handled, concerning the Word of Life- the life was manifested, and we have seen, and bear witness, and declare to you that eternal life which was with the Father and was manifested to us, that which we have seen and heard we declare to you, that you also may have fellowship with us, and truly our fellowship is with the Father and with the His Son Jesus the Christ. These things we write to you that your joy may be full."*

These verses are so appropriate for the events of this book. These are the eye witness accounts of the extraordinary events of God in my life that I want to share in order to encourage other believers. My purpose is to increase your faith in the power of

Christ in your life. These are the stories that have anchored my faith in never turning back to the darkness but continuing in light, His light, to the finishing of my faith.

My hope is that through these events you will begin to recognize His daily work in your life and give Him the praise for it. Psalm 34 is the pinnacle of my existence. *"I will bless the Lord at all times: His praise shall continually be in my mouth. My soul shall make its boast in the Lord: The humble shall hear of it and be glad. Oh magnify the Lord with me, and let us exalt His name together."*

If these stories increase your faith and move you to a higher praise of Him, then these words will have accomplished that which they were intended to do.

Blessings to you,
Don (Caleb) McCain
A messenger of the Lord Jesus Christ

Chapter 1
Saved From Eternal Death

I was 20 years old and in love.

I attended church with my girlfriend, whom I planned to marry. I really didn't believe all those *church* stories about Jesus. I only attended to please her.

My girlfriend, on the other hand, was a devout Christian, and she knew that to be unequally yoked was not God's way. She did the right thing. She broke it off with me.

I could not accept that her church beliefs were the real reason (I truly was clueless), so I parked across the street from her house night after night waiting to see the new guy who had taken my place. No one ever showed up, to take her out.

I called her, and she continued to say, "It's Jesus. He is the other man, and I cannot disappoint Him."

My friends wanted to help me out in the only way they knew how. We'd hang out all night, go to bars and get wasted. It didn't help.

I was hurting badly, so badly that I decided the only way to end the pain was to take my own life. I had it all planned out. I was going to take my car down the Interstate, crank it up to 100 miles per hour and hit an over pass.

It was a relief to think the pain of that broken relationship was finally going to end. The fateful night arrived, and off I went. I punched the accelerator harder, picked up speed, faster and faster. The overpass came into view. This was the end.

But something happened. Something deep down inside of me cried out. I don't know what to call it. Maybe it was fear, or sheer panic, but instinctively I knew that if I hit the bridge, the next moment I would be in hell.

I slowed the car down and pulled over to the side of the road. The sense of terror over the state of my eternal soul was overwhelming. I had already decided that this *Jesus* thing was just a man-made crutch for the weak, but now I wasn't so sure. There was a battle raging way down deep inside of me, and I knew I needed to make a choice. I just wasn't really sure what the choices were.

I meditated on this fear that had reared up inside of me as I drove back to my home - a three-bedroom mobile-home in a trailer park.

I went to my bedroom, undressed and crawled into bed. The longer I laid there, the more confused and angry I grew. I finally got so mad I cried out loud, "I can't live in this world and I can't leave this world. Nobody cares about me!"

At that moment I had one of the most dramatic experiences of my life. I heard an audible voice thunder in my room. It was loud, yet comforting.

"I have always loved you and I will never leave you nor forsake you."

Those words might sound familiar to you, but I didn't know there were verses in the Bible that said the same thing. (Deuteronomy 31:6, Hebrews 13:6, Joshua 1:5, just to name a few). What I did know was this was truly the voice of God.

My first impulse was repentance. I didn't think about it. I just responded.

"Oh my God, you *are* real! I am so sorry for the mess I've made of my life. I want you."

Immediately I felt the proverbial peace like a river flood over me. I didn't understand why, but I knew everything would be alright from that moment on. I lay back down and slept peacefully for the rest of the night.

It's true. His mercies are new every morning. I awoke a new man in Christ Jesus, full of peace and joy.

It's funny, but my thoughts turned to Him whom I knew nothing about, and the desire to know Him had replaced the loneliness in my heart for my former girlfriend. I found myself talking to God, just talking to Him. I wouldn't call it prayer, because I didn't know anything about praying, much less how to do it.

I picked up an old King James Bible I received as a high school graduation present and started reading. It was tough. I have a hard enough time with American English, but Elizabethan English was something else altogether. I guess I thought God just talked funny. But it's okay; at least He talks. I assumed I would figure Him out sooner or later.

All I knew was I was in love with Him. He had shed His love abroad in my heart, and I just responded to that love even though I didn't understand a word I was reading.

I was too new in the journey to know that only Spirit can reveal the Spirit. I found that out later.

Chapter 2
The Call

I stopped hanging out with my drinking buddies. Actually, they stopped hanging out with me after I shared this encounter with God. They felt sorry for me. They thought I had lost my mind because of this girl. But feeling sorry for me didn't equate to wanting to spend time with me.

My old friends were gone and I hadn't made any new friends. Over all, it was a pretty lonely time but I was alright with that. I had never felt this clean and safe in my entire life. I didn't have any flesh-and-blood friends to talk to, so I just talked to this invisible friend called Jesus. I couldn't see Him but I knew He was there.

One night while sleeping I had a bizarre dream, and in the dream I heard a knock at the door. When I opened the door, there stood Billy Graham. I said,

You're Billy Graham. He said, *And you're Don McCain. Won't you come?* I remembered watching Dr. Graham's crusades on TV when I was a boy and at the end of the service he would always say that. *Won't you come?*

In my dream I replied, *Yes.* It was as if I was a TV cameraman, filming the whole event.

The dream shifted and the next thing I saw was Dr. Graham and I, sitting on a white bench in the park. He was talking to me, and I knew he was teaching me about Jesus. There was no sound; just a knowing.

The dream shifted again and I had a camera shot view of a football coliseum. As the camera panned down through the crowd to the field I saw a long box and a pulpit with a speaker behind it. I thought, *This is a Billy Graham crusade.*

The sound came on and there was a close up of the speaker. It was *me,* with my arms stretched out, just like Billy Graham would do.

Here lies a man who gave his whole life for the Gospel of Jesus Christ, I said. I was giving his eulogy. I ended with my arms stretched out wide, saying, *Won't you come?*

I awoke, standing in the hall of that trailer with my arms stretched out, saying over and over, *Won't you come? Won't you come?*

I have never before or after walked in my sleep and I don't mind admitting, it scared me. I went back to my bed, pulled the covers over my head and slept that way till morning.

I forgot about the dream as soon as I awakened the next morning. I showered and dressed and went off to work, as usual. I worked as the manager in the men's and boys' clothing department at the brand new K-mart in Granite City, Illinois. I went about my daily routine; stocking shelves, making schedules, helping customers. I carried an armload of sports coats to a circular display stand and was arranging them by price point when I felt the presence of someone behind me.

I turned to see an old man standing there, just staring at me.

"So, God has called you to preach," he said.

"Not me," I replied.

"Are you sure God has not called you to preach?" the old man pressed.

I said, "Would you like to try on a sport coat?"

"I can do that," he replied.

I sized him up and slipped a jacket on him.

"Are you sure God has not called you to preach the Gospel?" he asked once again.

I just smiled and said, "No. I sell clothes."

Out of nowhere the old man said, "Tell me about the dream you had last night."

If I thought the conversation had been a little strange before, now I was sure of it. In fact, I was more than a little freaked out. I slowly removed the jacket and turned my back on the man. While I was hanging the jacket back up, he said, "I believe God has called you to preach the Gospel."

When I turned back around to deny it, he was gone. The little old man was just...gone! I ran all around the store looking for the old man, but he was nowhere to be found. I thought I was losing my mind.

That night I called my uncle who worked in Chicago, and asked if I could come and work for him. He wanted to know if I was in some kind of trouble.

I told him, "You have no idea of the trouble I'm in."

He told me to come on, so I did. I moved to Chicago and I started working for him at a loan company. He gave me the position of repo man. My job was to go and take stuff away from people...poor people.

I tried putting Jesus and the old man out of my thoughts, but it wasn't working too well. I had only been on the job for a couple weeks when I was sent to repossess a TV from a poor family in the inner city. When I got to the house, I saw a child, dirty and hardly clothed. I never made it inside.

I broke down and had a crying fit as the reality of abject poverty washed over me. I drove back to the office. I was still crying hard when I walked in. My uncle started tearing up and he asked what happened.

"God is calling me to preach His Gospel," I managed between snuffles. "I've got to go home now. I can't run any longer."

My uncle left the office with me to help me pack. I left for home that very hour.

Shiloh, Illinois was a little, one gas-pump town, and it was a good thing because by the time I got there I was out of gas. I pulled up to the fuel pump and Dale Hewitt, a guy I had gone to high school with, came up to pump the gas (that was before the days of self-service gas stations). He recognized me and reached through my window to give me a hug.

I'll admit his reaction to seeing me freaked me out just a little. I got out of the car and Dale hugged me all the more.

"Don McCain, God loves you," he said. "My mom and I have been praying for the last two years that you would come to Christ."

I began to cry again and told Dale, "I received Christ but don't know what to do next." He told me take my stuff home, get unpacked, then come to his house.

I did just that. I met him at his house. From that time on Dale and his mother began to teach me the Word.

Dale introduced me to several of his friends and we started hanging out together. Every night we'd study the things of God as a group. I was excited to find out how big God really is.

I am still discovering that to this very day.

One of my new friends bought a New American Standard Bible and gave it to me to study with. It was great! I could understand the English so much better than the King James Version.

One Sunday night Dale preached his first message. The whole gang was there. I don't remember what Dale preached about, but I remember the invitation time. I went forward. The pastor met me down at the front and asked if I wanted to get saved.

"No," I said. "I've already been saved."

The pastor looked confused and asked me why I had walked the aisle.

"I am supposed to preach the Gospel, just like Dale is doing," I replied.

The pastor turned to the congregation and said, "Well, we have another Dale on our hands."

✠✠✠

Don with his 1972 Camero, running from God.

The Charismatic renewal was in full swing as inter-denominational groups of people started meeting together to experience God more fully. The meetings we were involved with took place every Friday night at Scott Air Force Base.

I had fractured my left wrist while playing football, and the doctor had my arm in a removable cast (that is important to know for what happens next). I went to one of our Friday night meetings and experienced something entirely new.

The preacher declared that God is the same yesterday, today and forever. He said, "If you need a miracle or healing, He will do it today just as He did 2,000 years ago."

I listened as people testified about being prayed for and getting healed. It was pretty exciting.

That's when it happened.

The preacher said, "There is someone here tonight with a broken left wrist, and God is going to heal it."

I started looking around for the person he was talking about.

Coretta, Dale's mother, leaned over and said, "Don, that's you."

"No," I said. "He has someone planted in the group."

Coretta just laughed.

The preacher looked right at me and said, "Are you going to come up and get your healing or not?"

I slowly stood up and made my way to the front. I figured he had made a big mistake and was going to be embarrassed.

"Can we take that cast off?" he asked.

"We can," I answered. "But it will hurt pretty badly."

He removed the cast and grasped my hand as if we were just two guys shaking hands. He reminded me that Jesus is the same yesterday, today and forever.

"That's right," I agreed.

He said, "Will you stop squeezing my hand before you break it."

I was shocked. The pain was gone!

"I am healed," I cried out. "I am healed!"

The preacher told me to tell four people God had healed my wrist on the way back to my seat, and I was happy to comply.

My wrist was completely healed that night. To everyone's surprise, the very next week I was back out on the field, playing football.

That summer was a great time of discipleship, of laying a foundation of faith in our God and His miracle power that would carry me to places and peoples I would never have dreamed. This new God adventure made football seem less challenging.

I witnessed a second great miracle during a Nora Lam event. Nora spoke in broken English, but her testimony of God's deliverance from a Chinese prison camp was incredible. In the middle of her testimony she just stopped and ran to a crippled girl who was sitting beside me.

"I have one Boss and I must do what my Jesus tells me to do," Nora cried out. "Young girl, arise and be healed."

I heard and saw these twisted limbs cracking and popping. Her legs and arms straightened out and she stood up and walked.

After the meeting, I asked Coretta and Dale, "Where does the power to do these things come from?"

"Acts 1:8," they explained. "When the power of the Holy Ghost comes upon you the power of God will work through you."

They gave me a book, "Like a Mighty Wind" by Mel Tari, and told me to to go home and read it.

I did. I went home, climbed the stairs to my bedroom, turned on the light that hung from a cord and crawled into my small twin-size bed to read. I was just getting into Tari's testimony, when the latch came up on my window and it flew open. The room filled with light and I started speaking uncontrollably in some crazy language I didn't know or understand. The light flowed down the stairs, opened the back door and rushed out. My brother said it looked like lightning. My dad was sitting on the couch and called up the stairs to me, "What's going on up there?"

Once I regained control, I remembered Coretta telling us to check every experience we had against the Word of God. I grabbed my new Bible off the stand and let it fall open, hoping God would shed some light on what I had just experienced.

The pages fell open to Acts, Chapter 2, vs.1, and I begin to read. It said when the day of Pentecost had finally come they were all together in one place with one mind and a sudden mighty rushing wind came in and they all began to speak in tongues.

"That's it," I thought. "That's what just happened to me. It is true. He *is* the same yesterday, today and forever, for I too have experienced this same event, 2,000 years later."

Dale and I were growing quickly in the Word and in favor with men. I worked as an assistant manager at Union Clothing, a men's clothing store, and I told people on a daily basis about the power of God. One day some of the folks there challenged me on my radical faith.

"If God still produces miracles today, let's see one," they scoffed.

It was a beautiful sunny day. We were putting tables out in front of the store for a sidewalk sale. Without even thinking I told them it would rain at high noon. Of course, they all laughed.

I said it again, "God will make it rain at high noon."

I thought to myself, "What in the world did you just say?"

As the morning wore on my compatriots continued checking the clock.

"I don't see any rain clouds," one would laugh.

"It's not noon yet," I'd reply, like an uncontrolled boulder rolling down a hill, all the while thinking, "What am I doing?"

At about 11:20 that morning I spotted a small cloud in the distance. I told everyone it would be over us at noon and rain. They just laughed and shook their heads.

For the next 40 minutes we were busy with customers and stocking shelves with products. Everyone forgot about the time. No one paid any attention to the weather. We were all startled by a sudden clap of thunder. At that moment every eye in the store looked up at the clock.

It was high noon and it was raining on Main Street. Someone cried out, "Get the clothes in out of the rain!" but I shouted back, "Don't worry. It will only last one minute."

Everyone just stood there, astonished, and watched the clock. One minute later the rain stopped.

I was so thankful the Lord watched over my words and produced this miracle for His Glory. He had just proven to me, and others, He is the same yesterday, today and forever.

Chapter 3
Going to Bible College

Dale and I started praying about attending Bible college to prepare for the ministry. I had already completed two years of forestry school, but now that my life was headed in a new direction, I needed a different kind of education.

Our pastor was quite helpful in that endeavor. He arranged an interview for me with Union University in Jackson, Tennessee, while Dale set his sites on Christ For The Nations Institute in Dallas, Texas. Our time of training under his mother was over. It was time for us to take the next step on our journey of faith.

Off to Union I went.

I found great favor at Union University, with both students and teachers, and discovered a true friend and kindred spirit, Sam Hawkins. Sam and I were roommates, real brothers in the Lord and had many a great adventure. To paraphrase the Apostle John, if I wrote down all of our college adventures, it would fill a whole 'nuther book, so I'll just hit the highlights.

One of these adventures happened when a so-called faith healer came to town. There were big advertisements in the newspaper, but while Sam and I regularly held Bible studies in our dorm room and proclaimed the unchanging power of God, this fellow did not sit well with me. I told Sam I believed he was a fake and we needed to do something about it.

Sam walked powerfully in the gift of the word of knowledge. "We are not prepared enough to go up against the demonic spirit behind this person," he said.

"Alright," I reluctantly agreed. But later that afternoon, around the time the healing service was supposed to start at the civic center, I said to Sam, "Let's go get some ice cream."

We hopped in my car and I drove toward the civic center.

"I knew you were going to do this," Sam said.

There was a crossover walkway that allowed you to look down into the center of the auditorium, and that's where we went. I watched as the *healer* opened his suitcase and said, "Bring your money down here, put it in my suitcase and God will heal you."

To say I was angry would be an understatement. Sam knew it and began praying for God's protection. I said quietly under my breath, "In the name of Jesus, leave the stage or die." It was then that the guy looked up right at me.

I repeated quietly once again, "Leave or die."

The faith healer started screaming, "I'm sick, I have to leave."

He started wiping his hands frantically with his handkerchief. I said quietly, "You cannot wipe the blood of Jesus off your hands. Be gone or die." A woman close by grabbed his leg. She cried out, "I need my miracle."

"Leave me alone woman," he shouted. "I don't have time for you. I have to leave or I'm going to die!"

With that he quickly grabbed the suitcase of money and ran off the stage. It was so quiet you could have heard a pin drop, even though there were more than 3,000 people in that room.

I sighed a breath of relief and so did Sam. We won, or so we thought.

Then it happened. A blood-curdling scream came from down front. A woman began speaking in a horrifying man's voice.

"I will kill you all, for this!"

She kept repeating it over and over. No one moved.

She stood up, turned and looked straight at me. She began to curse me as she walked up the stairs toward me. She claimed she would kill me and everyone else in the place.

She got to the landing where I stood. Our gazes were fixed upon each other as she walked straight toward me. She started to open her mouth, but I grabbed her hands and said, "Jesus loves you."

She fell straight down to the ground at my feet. When she looked back up at me, her entire countenance had changed. She had been delivered.

"You cannot buy God's healing," we explained to those who were now filing out of the auditorium. "It is free. Go home. Talk to God about your need, and trust him."

✠✠✠

Sam and I had another friend we called Weird Mike. He was really out there in the Spirit realm. Most people would have called us Jesus freaks, but we could not hold a candle to the likes of Weird Mike. He was the Jesus freak to end all Jesus freaks.

I went with Mike to a prayer meeting one night. The group met in a family's upstairs bonus room. Mike didn't tell me much about this group, other than that I would enjoy myself. There were around forty people there when we showed up.

Chairs were arranged around the perimeter of the room, leaving an open area in the center. I assumed that's were the leader would minister from. The lady of the house stood up to welcome us, and to introduce the person who would be ministering that evening.

"Friends," she said. "Tonight we are honored to have one of our own Union University students to minister to us. Don McCain."

I was shocked!

Weird Mike had volunteered me without even asking me.

I turned to Mike and said, "What's this all about?"

"I was interested in seeing what the Holy Spirit would do on the spur of the moment," he grinned back at me.

I had not even brought my Bible.

I had a choice. I could retreat into myself and refuse to take the lead, or I could embrace the opportunity to be used by the Lord. I stood up, thanked the host and said, "Let's pray."

As we prayed I began to see things in the Spirit; someone struggling to breathe. I described what I was sensing out loud.

"Someone here is dying of lung cancer and God is going to heal you tonight," I heard myself say.

A woman stood and said, "It is my father."

"Bring him to the center of the room," I told her. "I'll lay hands on him and pray."

As he came forward I could actually hear him struggling for breath. He sat down in a chair in the center of the room. As soon as I laid hands on him, before I could utter a single word in prayer, everyone in the room could hear his breathing change from labored to normal.

He was instantly healed.

I continued sharing things I saw in the Spirit.

"Someone has a son that left, like the prodigal and you have been praying for a long time for him to come home," I said. "Tonight, around midnight, he will call you. He will ask if he can come home, and he'll want to come back to Jesus."

Amazing things continued to happen that evening, many of which were confirmed later. The boy called at midnight. He returned home and came back to Jesus. The old man visited his doctor, whose report verified that the lung cancer was gone. He was completely whole.

Years later, we discovered that the fire department had been called to that address while we prayed, because neighbors thought the roof was on fire. The fire department decided not to disturb us for two reasons: first, because the fiery glow settled above the roof, not on it, and second, because they were simply in awe and quite frankly afraid to come to the door. The firemen just watched until the supernatural glow left. I found that out after talking with a fireman who knew all about that night's strange fire call.

While still at the university, a student asked me to pray that God would send him a hundred dollars to pay a school bill. I did, and a couple of days later he received a hundred dollars in the mail. He got so excited he told a friend about it.

"I could use a hundred dollars, too," his friend said. "Let's get him to pray for me."

They hunted me down, we prayed and a few days later there was another hundred dollars in his mail box. I said to them, "Hey guys, I need a hundred dollars, too."

They prayed for me and, you guessed it, in a couple days, a hundred dollars showed up in my mail box. Of course, it wasn't just about the money, but God provided for me so many times and in so many ways while I was in college I just can't say enough about it. But the greatest gift I received from God during my college years had nothing to do with money.

A number of us hung out together, including a young lady from Chicago, Patti Madderom. My, oh my, she was something I had never encountered before. I had girlfriends before, but never one that I was so comfortable with, one that I laughed so much with. She was a nursing student and I called her Florence Nightingale or Flo.

Sam didn't think she was right for me, but I think that was because all the time I spent with her was cutting into our buddy time.

This young lady and I grew closer as time passed. One day as I was praying, the Lord spoke to the depths of my heart. "This is the one I have chosen for you."

I was happy, but scared.

She's the one God has chosen for me. What does that mean? Marriage?

I went to find Sam.

"Sam, we have to talk," I said.

"There's nothing to talk about," Sam shrugged his shoulders. "God told me she is the one chosen for you."

I stood there with my mouth hanging open like a large-mouth bass.

"What did you say?" I stammered.

"You heard me," Sam replied. "As I was praying for you about Patti, God told me it was alright. He said He had chosen her for you and that I should just be okay with it. I am, so let's get on with other things."

Soon after, on a clear spring day, I asked Patti to go for a walk with me around the campus and we ended up at the baseball field. I led her over to a nearby stack of concrete blocks and lifted her up to sit on them.

"There is something I need to talk to you about," I stammered. I don't remember anything else that came out of my mouth, but it must have been real good, because when it was over, she said, "Yes!"

To this day Patti is the best gift God has ever given me. We are MFEO, *made for each other*.

The summer before I met Patti, I injured myself at work. I fell down a flight of stairs going to the basement at the clothing store and broke my right knee cap in half. I hobbled around campus on crutches the entire fall semester, hoping to make it to winter break to have surgery. Sam and I routinely had prayer meetings in our dorm with a bunch of other guys, and we asked God to heal my knee.

Winter break came, and I went home. Before long I found myself in the hospital preparing for surgery - they wanted to remove my knee cap and replace it with a disc. Two hours before surgery my knee started feeling warm, almost hot. The joy of the Lord came over me and I began to laugh.

An orderly came in to prep my leg for surgery.

"I don't need surgery," I told him. "My leg is healed."

He gave me a skeptical look, nodded and said, "I'll be right back."

To my surprise, the orderly soon returned with a wheelchair and off to x-ray we went. It turned out it wasn't my confession that motivated him. The doctor simply wanted another set of x-rays before surgery.

They pumped dye in my knee and the x-ray technician did his thing. I sat in those glamorous backless pj's common to hospitals, in a frigid waiting room while they developed the x-rays. It seemed to take forever, as if they were intentionally trying to wear me down. Whether real or imagined, it was working. I was worn out by the time the surgeon stepped into the room and asked me if I wanted to see the pictures.

I nodded and followed him into the x-ray development room. The surgeon held up an x-ray.

"These are your old pictures," he said as he pointed out a quarter-inch gap between the two halves of my knee cap.

"This," he said as he placed another x-ray in front of the light, "is your new picture."

The knee cap in this x-ray was whole, without a scratch on it.

I looked from the x-ray to the surgeon, then back at the x-ray.

"So, what does this mean?" I asked.

"It means you don't need surgery," he replied, a frown creasing his face. "But I would like to do exploratory surgery, just to find out how this thing happened, if you don't mind."

"Seriously? You want to operate on a perfectly good knee," I said.

"No," he sighed. "I guess not."

"What should I tell the school administration when I return for spring semester?"

"Tell them you had a deranged knee," the surgeon laughed. "I'll back you up."

Then he got thoughtful for a moment.

"You said you were a preacher didn't you?"

"Yes," I replied.

"I lose more patients that way," he said as he shook my hand and walked away.

Patti's mom had a picture of the two of us and sent it to the local newspaper in her home town to announce our engagement. Her family invited me to join them for Easter and I accepted. During the six-hour drive from Shiloh to Chicago I had another God encounter.

There were two options that would take me to my destination: I-57 or I-55. I prayed about it and chose the I-57 route. When I arrived at the entrance ramp to the Interstate, I saw a hitchhiker with his thumb out. While I don't advise people to pick up hitchhikers, I felt the urging of the Holy Spirit and stopped to pick him up. I figured I'd witness to him about the Lord on the way to Chicago.

I asked him where he was headed.

"Mattoon," he said, "back to campus."

I thought about just dropping him off at the exit, but instead I carried him all the way to his dorm. As I headed back out of town I saw another hitchhiker. Once again I pulled over. The guy ran to the door and leaned in through the open window."

"Don?" he said.

"Glenn?" I answered, just as surprised.

The hitchhiker was Patti's younger brother, making his way home for Easter. What were the odds of that happening?

I realized it was all arranged by God; every detail orchestrated by the Lord. We had no cell phones to make it happen; no means of setting it up before hand. It was just another daily miracle in the life of a believer.

During my last semester in college, Patti and I began to plan our wedding for the following autumn. When I preached revival meetings I introduced her as my bride-to-be, and one church even threw us a wedding shower.

Those meetings were held mostly in small farming communities and the folks were just wonderful. The Lord performed great wonders in these small churches, but the most miraculous of all was when someone accepted Christ as their personal Lord and Savior.

It was around this time that I met a young evangelist named Sammy Tippet. He had written a book, *God's Love in Action*, which had a great impact on me. Sammy had started a ministry in Uptown Chicago during the Jesus movement, and through his book I felt the Lord leading me to go to Chicago and take his place.

Sammy had followed the Lord to Eastern Europe where he was ministering to believers behind the Iron Curtain by smuggling in Bibles. That was a dangerous ministry in those days, but God always helped Sammy and his team cross the border without the Bibles being discovered.

When I talked to Patti about my desire to minister in Chicago, she got excited. Her family lived on the Southside of Chicago, and it would mean being close to her home and her family. But even though I felt the stirring from the Holy Spirit, I still had some misgivings. I wasn't sure how this whole 'going to Chicago' was going to work out. I didn't know anyone working in ministry there. All I had to go on was Sammy's book.

Sam, my roommate, was also concerned.

"You can't just go barging in up there like a bull in a China shop," he said. "You need to have an open door; a word of confirmation; something. You just can't take off."

I knew Sam was right, but this urging from the Holy Spirit was just so strong. I sought counsel from Dr. Aggie, the Dean of students and religious affairs.

"Wait on the Lord to open the door," he advised. "And keep doing what the Lord has put in front of you to do."

It was good advice, and I agreed.

It was only a few days later when Dr. Aggie called me to his office. He introduced me to Pastor Tim Wills, who had just started pastoring in the inner city of Chicago.

"I need a youth pastor to work along side me," he said.

Chapter 4
New Beginnings

The school year ended. Patti's parents came and took her home. I packed up my stuff and headed out to join Pastor Tim.

He introduced me to the board of elders who appeared genuinely glad for me to be there. Tim and I started fixing up the basement in his house. It was to be Patti's and my first home.

I started a Bible study group with a bunch of Catholic kids. I loved it. Tim loved it. The board of elders did not love it.

As unthinkable as it was to my mind, they asked me to leave. It seems they didn't want Catholic boys hanging out in their church building.

Tim was crushed. So was I. The situation had me second-guessing myself. Was it possible that I missed God? It all *seemed* so right.

A few days later, Tim asked me to meet with another pastor who wanted to start a new work in the inner city.

"He doesn't have a board, and he's excited about the possibility of you joining him," Tim told me.

That's when I met Pastor Jim Queen, who was starting a ministry in Uptown Chicago. A group of East Texas Bible College students were helping him start the ministry by working as summer missionaries. I was the oldest of the group, and the only one other than Jim who was called to preach.

Jim hosted an organizational meeting for the new work and had invited a special minister to stop by and encourage the group. He was going to give us pointers on how to work on the streets of Chicago.

The 'special minister' was Sammy Tippit who was surprised to see me there.

"If you want to start a church in the inner city of Chicago, just turn this guy loose and let him preach," Sammy told Jim. "He's as bold as a lion, and walks in the power of God. Give him opportunities and you will get a church going."

That's all Jim needed to hear. He held Sunday services and I spoke anywhere and everywhere he wanted. I spoke at the Boys' Club. I spoke at the Kiwanis Club. I preached on street corners, at block parties, at ball games and wherever else the Holy Spirit opened a door.

Those were exciting times. Young people got saved. Their parents got saved. We saw whole families come to the Lord. By the time summer came to an end, we had a large congregation. That ministry, which is now known as Uptown Baptist Church, is more than 35 years old, and is still going strong.

I don't want anyone to get the idea that what we were doing in the inner city of Chicago was a walk in the park. It was a rough area, and it could be dangerous if you weren't careful. We always worked in teams. No one was supposed to be on the streets alone.

As fate, or the Holy Spirit, would have it, I ended up on the streets alone one day. I was running an errand for Jim. I turned the corner on Sunnyside Mall, an area notorious for gang violence, and coming toward me was the leader of the Latin Kings.

I shifted to the left to move out of his way. He shifted to his right and kept coming straight at me. I moved back over to my right, and he shifted back to his left. It was plain we were going to have a close encounter, whether I wanted to or not.

Once he got close, he pulled a gun, cocked it and put the barrel to my forehead.

"Priest, I am going to blow you away," he said.

"Go ahead," I replied. "You'll just send me where I want to go anyway."

He just stood there, dumbfounded.

"I have never seen anyone who was not afraid to die," he said. "Tell me why."

For the next hour I told him my story. By the time I finished, I had a new friend.

I became the chaplain to his gang.

Once my new friend left, I was approached by another man from across the street, who turned out to be a plain clothes police officer.

"I saw and heard the whole thing," he said. "I just want you to know I had your back the whole time."

"Well, when were you planning on doing something?" I asked.

"After he shot you," the officer laughed. "Seriously, the whole police force has been watching you guys. We're here to help if you need us. It just doesn't look like you need any help."

Sunnyside Mall was a magnet for gang activity

The Magnolia Street area was in serious disrepair.

We did everything we could to attract kids and their families. We held back-alley events and front-street events. We played games with the street kids. We passed out food. We arranged for housing, clothing and furniture for the displaced and the down-and-out. The community was changing, and as one local bank manager said, it was all because of one man - Pastor Jim Queen.

Jim was a great leader, and he became a big brother to me. He had the gift of organization, and God gave him favor everywhere he went. He helped people get bank loans to start new business. He helped move people into apartments. He helped families get established. He often worked far into the night and he never seemed to tire of helping people.

To this day, he is one of the most respected men in the Uptown community. When we started working there many of the business buildings were empty and boarded up. The neighborhood homes were neglected and in disrepair. The average family income was less than $2,000 per year. Today both the community and local businesses thrive. What a difference one man of God can make.

It wasn't just the residents of Uptown that got blessed. God's provision extended to Patti and me as well.

Shortly before we were married I sustained a serious injury. I was helping some guys move an old upright piano from a second floor apartment. It was big, and it was heavy. I arrived a little late and they decided to get started without me.

I walked up just as they were coming down the stairs; two guys on the upside of the piano and one guy below. Suddenly, the guys above the piano lost their grip. The guy below the piano ran for his life, but fell into the wall at the end of the stairs as the piano barreled down straight for him.

I stepped over him, braced one hand against the wall and extended the other hand straight out towards the piano. I looked like Superman standing there protecting that defenseless guy. It worked too, sort of. I stopped the piano. But I crushed my left shoulder in the process.

I went to see a specialist who told me I needed surgery to repair the damage. I didn't want surgery and fought against it for as long as I could. I knew it would be expensive, and we didn't have insurance.

Besides, I kept thinking about how God had miraculously healed my knee cap. Surely He could do it again. But it didn't happen that way.

The pain got so bad I had to go into the clinic to see if I could get help.

I saw the same specialist who just shook his head at me.

"I guess you're ready for that surgery now," he said.

"Yes, I am," I admitted.

It was a little humbling, but God had shown us time after time that He was our source. We weren't on any church payroll. The ministry we served had no money to pay us, but every week we received checks in the mail from people we didn't even know. We never missed our rent, utility payments or a meal. God had always provided, but this was major surgery.

No insurance; no money. What did we do?

We just trusted Him.

Between the operation and rehab, the total cost exceeded $20,000. That's a lot of money today. Back then it was exorbitant.

When the bill finally arrived, Patti and I both did a double-take.

Zero. The bill said we owed nothing; nada; zilch.

How could this be? The explanation we got was that the surgeon used the procedure he had performed on me as a textbook example for a class he taught.

Thirty years later we found out that the surgeon had paid the bill himself. That is the unmerited favor of our God pouring out on our behalf, just because He loves us. There is no other way to explain that kind of miracle.

Don & Patti's wedding, October 3, 1976 with Jim Queen.

It was during our sojourn in the city that I had to conduct my first funeral for a young man who was killed in a gang war. The funeral was tough, but the events surrounding the end of the service provided another opportunity for God to show up.

The Gaylords, an Appalachian white gang, had a rumble with the Latin Kings and lost a young man in the process. Once the funeral service was over, the funeral home director pulled me aside and told me to look outside. There, across the street, were the Latin Kings.

"Call the police," I told him. "Tell them we need an escort to the grave site."

While the funeral director made the call, I walked outside and across the street to the leader of the Latin Kings.

"There will be no rumble today," I told him. "This is a day to show respect. I would expect the Gaylords to do the same if it were one of your guys, so stand down."

"Priest," the leader of the Kings said, "you are something else. For you we will go home. We'll do this another day."

Maybe he really did respect me. Maybe it was the power of the Holy Spirit working in the situation. Maybe it was the fact that the police showed up just at that moment. I think maybe it was the Holy Spirit moving the police to show up at just the right time. Whatever the reason, the Latin Kings left, and the police escorted the funeral possession to the grave site.

✠✠✠

Eventually our season of work in the Windy City came to an end, but not before we trudged through one of the worst winters on record. Temperatures dropped down to 50 degrees below zero. It was definitely not the kind of weather a southern boy was accustomed to.

And Patti was expecting our first child.

Chapter 5
Moving On

Spring came, and we were on the move. We were called to the suburbs to pastor our first church - First Baptist Church of Dolton Illinois, in the same town where Patti's parents lived.

Pastoring is a fulltime job, but in many cases it doesn't provide a fulltime income. In addition to shepherding the small flock at First Baptist, I was also the assistant manager of a shoe store and worked at the local food preservative plant.

You can only maintain that kind of schedule when you're 25 years old.

Our time at First Baptist was short, but interesting. I volunteered as a follow-up pastor for the PTL Club, and I received a call from them saying a group of Catholics meeting at the local Lutheran

Church was looking for someone to teach them about the Holy Spirit. Although our schedule was already maxed out, I accepted the challenge.

Nina Paradi headed up the feisty little group of elderly believers. We visited in the home of a husband and wife who were both almost blind. I had never seen cataracts before.

"Does it hurt?" I asked in my naivety.

"No," they answered, "but we can't see very well."

I had no idea how to proceed with such a need, so I just did what I had read in the Bible that Jesus did. I reached out my hands and placed them on both their eyes at the same time.

"In the name of Jesus, *see*," I said.

Streams of something milky-white flowed down both sets of cheeks. Their eyes became clear. They both could see clearly.

If I thought Nina was going to be surprised, I had *another think coming*, as we say in the South. She was not shocked at all, but she appeared to be pleased that we had come with her.

Nina's group met secretly at the Lutheran Church for fear that the local Catholic priest would disapprove of their charismatic tendencies. You can imagine the shock on everyone's face the night Father Norbert sauntered into the meeting place. From their downcast expressions it seemed they were bracing for excommunication.

I greeted Father Norbert and asked him to join us.

Father Norbert was very polite...and very Irish. He pulled up a chair as if this were the most natural thing in the world. This man of God had to be at least in his 70's. He had been in the ministry longer than I had been alive. I deferred to his age and experience.

"Father Norbert," I said, "why don't you share Jesus tonight?"

"No," he replied. "I came to hear you share Jesus."

I mark that meeting as one of the greatest moments in my life. The man had such humility; I have prayed many times since meeting him, *Lord help me to be more like Father Norbert.*

We visited frequently after that, and as I got to know him, his great love for our Lord became more and more obvious. I can't tell you how much I grew spiritually as a result of our relationship.

✠✠✠

Those were busy days. We were involved in a multitude of ministries on the south side of Chicago. In addition to teaching at Nina's group and pastoring my own congregation, we started a coffee house with another young ministry couple, Jim and Mary Woods.

After all, Jesus said *Go into all the world and preach the Gospel.* I assumed it was up to us to get that job done.

Don preaching at a park event in South Holland
Chicago southside. 1977

One night at our church Patti, Jim and I were down at the altar. We prayed and shared about our encounters with God.

"I've never encountered God the way you have," Jim said.

"Well, you can," I replied, and we started to pray for a divine encounter for Jim, right then as we knelt by the altar.

After a moment Jim said, "Don, did you just put your hand on my shoulder?"

"No," I said. "I'm over here."

"It wasn't me," Patti said. "I'm over here."

Jim had just experienced a physical manifestation of the Holy Spirit. It startled him so much he was afraid to drive himself home. That night was a great faith builder in Jim's life.

✠✠✠

The phone rang. Nina was on the other end of the line.

"We haven't heard from Leonard in several days and we're starting to get worried about him," she said. "Would you go check on him?"

That was not my idea of a good time. I knew where Leonard lived and it was not in a safe part of town. On top of that, Leonard was in his 70's and pretty frail. I was afraid he might have died from a heart attack or some other natural cause. As it turned out, it would have been less frightening if he had died.

The house was completely dark when I arrived. The porch light was off. There wasn't a single light glowing in any window.

I knocked at the door.

No answer.

I tried the door knob.

It turned, too easily, and the door swung open.

I allowed my eyes to grow accustomed to the dark, stuck my head inside the door, and walked in. As I feared, there was Leonard, slumped over in his easy chair. I thought he was dead.

As I knelt down in front of him, he raised his head and looked me straight in the eye, but I knew it wasn't Leonard looking at me. Whatever it was, it had a wild, crazed look that I've never seen in human being's eyes before.

He opened his mouth, and with a voice that came straight from the pit of hell said, "I'm going to kill you...and Leonard."

The hair on the back of my head stood at attention.

Leonard is demon-possessed! The thought flittered through my mind. *Great, now what do I do?*

I was no stranger to demonic activity. I had seen their obvious work, but I had never encountered a real demon before. Not like this. Not an actual face-to-face encounter.

I mustered up all the courage I could find, looked into its eyes and said, "Come out of Leonard."

The spirit just smiled and said, "No."

No? Now what do I do, I thought.

"Come out!" I commanded again.

"You can't make me," the demon taunted back.

In my spirit I heard the Holy Spirit say, *Use the name of Jesus.*

"I command you to come out of Leonard now, in the name of Jesus!"

"No," the demon refused, but there was less certainty in its voice.

I raised my hand over Leonard's head.

"What are you doing?" the demonic voice whined.

"I'm going to lay hands on Leonard in the name of Jesus," I replied, far more calmly than I felt.

"No! Don't torment me. Don't torment me," the voice pleaded.

I pressed my hand down onto Leonard's chest.

"No!" the voice wailed.

I watched the fires of hell fade from Leonard's eyes. As they became clear again Leonard gained awareness and was startled to see me standing over him.

"What happened," he croaked, his throat parched.

"You don't remember?" I said. "You had a demon controlling you."

We talked for a while. Leonard told me his story and I shared the Word with him. There was a bare light bulb hanging from an electrical cord from the ceiling in his bedroom. Leonard told me that every night when he turned that light off, a little green creature would enter his room, jump up and turn the light back on. He would turn it back off and the green thing would turn it back on. Eventually he just left the light on all night. Subtle surrenders to the Adversary can open the door to demonic oppression and even possession. That's what happened to Leonard.

"Demons don't like to be evicted from their dwelling places, and if given half a chance they will return," I told him.

I spent considerable time explaining how he could make sure the demon stayed away. It was time well spent. The very next night Leonard would have to fight the battle for himself.

The evening after his deliverance the green thing returned and tried to grab the light. Leonard cried out, "In the name of Jesus, be gone!"

"It vanished in a puff and never returned," Leonard told me later.

That man discovered the truth of the Gospel that *greater is He that is in me than He that is in the world.*

✠✠✠

Patti and I continued doing evangelistic work with local churches in the region, sometimes with unexpected results.

We were invited by a Baptist congregation to come and teach on the subject of; *Jesus is the same, yesterday, today and forever.* At the conclusion of the service I invited anyone who wanted to receive a blessing from the Lord to come forward and be prayed for.

At that time is was not a common experience for people to experience the spiritual phenomenon now known as being *slain in the spirit*...particularly not in a Southern Baptist church. Folks lined up in front of the pulpit and I went down the line, touching them on the forehead and praying for them. They started falling over, one after another.

It was not what I expected to happen, but pride started to well up in me.

Look what I'm doing, I thought.

At that moment the next person I prayed for did not fall.

I prayed a little harder, and even gave that person a slight nudge, but...nothing. I was about to give a harder nudge, when the Holy Spirit spoke to me.

"What are you doing?" He said. "Move on."

Humbled, I obeyed and moved on to the next person in line. That one fell down under the power of the Holy Spirit; as did all of the rest of the people in the line.

Once I reached the end of the line I heard the Holy Spirit say, "Turn and look at the one left standing."

As I looked at the man, he fell down under the power of the Spirit. That's when I learned it's not about me. It's about Him.

✠✠✠

It was time for our first child to be born. We went to St. Francis Hospital on the north side of Chicago for Patti's check–ups and the eventual delivery. We were as excited as any expectant young parents could be. Everything appeared just fine - but it was not.

The delivery went well and we held our sweet, beautiful little girl, Erin Kendra, in our arms. What a gift from God!

Our joy was short-lived. Within a few days the doctors told us Erin needed surgery to correct a blockage between her large and small intestines. We laid hands on her and asked the Lord to heal her. We had witnessed His healing power so many times before. Surely this would be another such glorious example of His great power.

However, Erin was not miraculously healed. The doctors explained that this was a very difficult surgery as many tiny blood vessels were involved. We agreed to go forward with the surgery and trusted her into the Lord's care. We all waited and watched to see whether the surgery would be a success. Then on her ninth day of life, Erin began to struggle for breath. In an attempt to save her life the doctors rushed her in for emergency surgery. When they opened her up, she flew away into the arms of Jesus.

It was a gloomy, rainy day in Chicago. Patti and I waited with her mother, hoping for good news from the surgeons. The news we hoped for and prayed for didn't come. Instead the doctor walked into the waiting room and told us, "I'm sorry, but your baby did not make it."

We were in shock; questions crowding our minds. How could this be? How could God take our sweet baby girl away from us, when we had given up so much to follow Him? We just stood in the middle of that big, empty room, with disbelief gripping our hearts like a vise.

A sudden ray of sunlight pierced through the clouds and burst through the window, embracing our family with an inexpressible light and warmth. We experienced an unbelievable closeness to God at that moment.

"That is the angels, coming to carry Erin home," I said.

That was the deepest kind of pain I have personally ever experienced. I honestly don't know how people survive this kind of pain without God in their lives.

Christian television broadcasting pioneer, Jerry Rose, was ministering in revival at our church during that time. He informed the church about the loss of our baby. Not only did he come to console us, Jerry preached Erin's funeral; his first funeral. He gave Patti and me a gift of $500 from WCFC-TV Channel 38, Chicago's first Christian television station. He encouraged us to get away, just the two of us, and be alone with the Lord.

Patti's father insisted on paying for the funeral, and he also encouraged us to go away and care for each other. We needed that.

Together we mourned the loss of our sweet Erin, but life goes on. We returned to the church and got back into the routine of ministry. We didn't understand why the Lord took our baby, and still don't, but we do understand that He was with us through the whole process. He never left us nor did He forsake us. As the old song goes, He was there all the time.

A year later, our son Samuel Patrick was born in our apartment with the help of our home delivery doctor. Finally, we had a baby we could hold in our arms and keep. Our joy was overflowing. Sam likes to think of himself as our oldest child, and he is our firstborn son, but we still think often about Erin. We long for the day when we will join her with our Lord forever. The experience of losing a child helped prepare us for the many funerals we would preside over in the years to come. When others lost children, we could truly say we understood how they felt. We could share the Father's love with them, knowing that He too lost a child.

I knew there were some Southern Baptist pastors in northern Illinois who were becoming annoyed with me, but I didn't really know how much until after the next revival meeting I preached. It was in a church near Springfield, Illinois.

Every night of the revival I encouraged the congregation to bring anyone who was sick to the Sunday afternoon meeting, and I would pray for God to heal them. I had taught all week on the doctrine of the work of faith, and that God is the same today as

He was yesterday, and He will be the same tomorrow.

When I arrived at the church on Sunday afternoon there was already a line of sick people stretching outside the building. The pastor and I prayed and laid our hands on the sick as the Word of God instructs, and watched as God healed people of all manner of illness.

If we had just contented ourselves with praying for the sick in that one little church, it might not have been a big issue. But God performed one special miracle during that service that changed the whole direction of our ministry.

A woman approached me and said, "My father is lying in a hospital bed, dying. Will you pray for him to be healed?"

I took out my handkerchief and poured oil on it. "Let's pray a prayer of agreement that he will recover and then go lay the handkerchief on him. Watch as God does the rest," I said.

It didn't take long after the meeting was over for news of what I'd done to burn up the pastors' grapevine. To my amazement, I started getting telephone calls from Baptist preachers asking me to leave the denomination.

I was devastated. I thought what I was doing was common among believers and especially ministers of the Gospel.

One pastor really chewed me out for my actions.

"I can't believe you would do such a thing as give that woman an oil-soaked handkerchief!" he sputtered.

"Well," I replied, "that's what the Apostle Paul did and the woman's father was raised up from his death bed. I figure, if it's good enough for Paul, it's good enough for me."

He hung up on me.

After much prayer, and to prevent dissention within the Body of Christ, we decided to leave our position with First Baptist Church of Dolton. Looking back, I was too young for such a responsibility anyway.

The First Assembly of God church was located right across the street from First Baptist. The pastor there felt our beliefs were more in line with the core beliefs of the Assembly, and suggested we come and visit. Within a few weeks, Patti and I joined with the Assemblies of God, which lead us into a whole new set of adventures.

✠✠✠

First Assembly of God in Collinsville Illinois, near my old stomping grounds, was looking for a youth pastor and called me for an interview. We were a great fit. The church took to us and we took to the church. The senior pastor totally released me to move in the Spirit during church services with the youth and in the community.

We started a ministry in the high school involving youth pastors of all denominations. We'd gather during the lunch period and invite the students to come and ask us questions about the Bible. This sparked a number of lively conversations.

"All it takes to get into heaven is just knowing that Jesus is the Son of God," one young lady argued.

"So you believe Satan will go to heaven?" I asked.

"Of course not," she replied.

"Well, doesn't he know Jesus is the Son of God?"

She just stood there for a moment with her mouth open.

"What more do you need to go to heaven?" she finally asked.

"It's not enough to just know Jesus is the Son of God," I explained. "The Bible says the devils believe and tremble. You must accept Him as your personal Lord and Savior and believe He died on the cross for your sins."

She prayed the sinner's prayer right then. It was a glorious moment, and just one of many we experienced during those times.

✠✠✠

One morning the pastor asked me to go and pray for a church member who was about to undergo cancer surgery. I arrived at the hospital a couple of hours before surgery was scheduled and encouraged her with some stories that I hoped would build her faith. I ended our time together with the scripture verse, *Jesus is the same yesterday, today, and forever.*

I laid hands on her and prayed that the surgeon would find no trace of cancer, but would instead find scalpel marks as evidence that the Great Physician had already removed the cancerous growth.

The orderlies came in to take her into surgery, and I moved to the waiting room. It was an hour before the surgeon walked into the room with a bemused look on his face.

"We have witnessed something most unusual," he tried his best to explain to us. "When we opened her up, the cancer was already gone. It looked like there was a scalpel mark around the area, but it was perfectly healed."

I told him that was exactly what we had prayed for moments before they took her to surgery. I don't know if the doctor believed me or not. He looked quite perplexed. But he was happy for the patient.

✠✠✠

Football was a favorite youth group activity, but it's not a great idea to let the kids play after it gets dark, as Patti and I discovered one Wednesday night. One of the boys walked back to the huddle with blood gushing from his mouth and his two front teeth missing. Fortunately, we found the two teeth and off we went to the hospital.

The emergency room nurse told us that if the teeth were not transplanted within forty-five minutes, they would die. Not forty-five minutes from now, mind you; forty-five minutes from the time of the accident. The hospital staff helped us find an after-hours dentist and we headed out again.

The dentist didn't think the teeth could be salvaged. Too much time had already expired.

"Just do it," I said, "and we'll rely on God for the results."

I prayed for the power of God to help the dentist replant the teeth and that they would live as a testimony of God's greatness.

Two weeks passed. One tooth was gleaming white but the other was a dull gray. The boy went back for a check-up and the dentist told him he would likely lose that tooth.

"No, I won't," the boy replied. "God is going to be glorified. He will make both teeth live."

The boy was right. Within a week the tooth began to regain its luster. Little by little they got whiter and whiter, then...well, you can guess the rest of that story.

✠✠✠

There was a wonderful older woman in our church that everyone called, "Grandma." She truly was a grandmother of the faith. She lived in a retirement center, and each week a member of the staff would drop by and visit with her.

One morning when it was my turn, I found Grandma in excellent health but poor spirits.

"Grandma, what's wrong?" I asked.

"Week after week you boys come here and pray for me to live on and on," she replied. "Just how old do I have to be before you let me go? When will you start praying with me for what I want, instead of asking me to pray for what you want?"

"Well, Grandma, what is it you want me to pray for?"

"I have lived a full and wonderful life," she said. "I think it is time for me to go home to be with Jesus. That's what I want you to pray for."

I admit to being a little surprised. I had never heard such a prayer request before. But I knew she was speaking from her heart. I apologized for being insensitive to her needs and desires, then prayed with her that the Lord would take her home that day."

"Thank you," she breathed a sigh of relief. We visited for a while longer, then I left and drove back to the church.

When I stepped into the office I heard our secretary crying.

"What's wrong?" I asked.

"The retirement center just called," she sniffed. "Grandma Lindsey just passed away."

I couldn't help myself. I just started laughing.

"What is wrong with you, Pastor Don?" the secretary shook her head in disbelief. "Didn't you hear what I said? Grandma just died!"

"Praise the Lord!" I replied. "That is the very thing she and I prayed for this morning."

When Sunday morning rolled around Pastor Phil told the congregation what had happened, and added that if anyone wanted to pass, just call on Pastor Don to pray for you.

"Don must be the Dr. Kevorkian of the church world," he quipped.

Everyone had a good laugh over it, but I've never had anyone else take him up on that request.

✠✠✠

We were still not over the loss of our first child, so it was not uncommon for me to get up in the middle of the night to check on our infant, Sam. I'd ease over to his crib as he lay sleeping and just rest my hand on his chest to make sure he was still breathing. I'm sure a lot of young parents can relate.

One evening when I placed my hand on Sam's little chest, it felt wet. I turned on the light and discovered the liquid was blood. Sam was bleeding from his nose.

I cried out for Patti. She jumped out of bed, frantic. Neither of us had any experience with such a situation and didn't know what to do. I called my mother, who quoted Ezekiel 16:6 to me: *I saw you lying in your blood and I said live, live.*

I turned to Sam and spoke those words over him. The bleeding stopped instantly.

We discovered that just as Jeremiah 1:12 states, *God watches over His word to perform it.* God's word is life to those who find it. Throughout the years I have seen that particular word never fail. Sam is now 35 and a father of three sons of his own.

Chapter 6
Missing God

Every day we miss God in one way or the other. Some misses are bigger than others, and have greater consequences. Some mistakes are just huge and take a while to work through.

Our pastor at First Assembly took a new church in Florida. In the Assemblies of God, when a new pastor comes in, a new youth pastor is put in place. We loved this church, and while God had done a great work among the youth and our community, we were being pushed out of the nest.

Capitol Hill Assembly of God in Oklahoma City offered us a position as youth pastors, and we jumped at it. Capitol Hill was a great church. It had a great pastor and great kids. It was the perfect position, the kind that youth pastors dreamed about. We had it made!

We only stayed for nine months.

Two things conspired to rob us of our time there: my best friend in New Orleans, who encouraged us to move there; and members of Capitol Hill who kept saying I was ready to be a Senior Pastor.

Really, there was only one thing that robbed us of a great run in Oklahoma; my pride.

It certainly wasn't because we didn't experience the power of God moving on our behalf at Capitol Hill. One memorable event occurred while we were on an outing with the teens. We traveled to a state park that had an outcropping of huge rock formations. The area was gorgeous and the rock cliffs were magnificent. The only problem was the pastor's son David, who was just a bit too adventurous.

We followed the trail all the way to the highest point before I noticed we were missing a couple guys.

"There he is, Pastor Don," one of the kids pointed at the cliff face.

David was attempting to climb up the ninety degree rock formation freestyle, and meet us at the top. Patti and I ran to the cliff's edge, laid down and looked over. I stretched my arm as far as I could but couldn't quite reach him.

I looked into his eyes and he looked in mine.

"I can't make it," he wheezed. Then he let go.

He fell more than 50 feet, straight down to the rocks below.

We all ran down the trail as fast as we could, praying with every step. He was still breathing when we finally reached him. He was unconscious.

Everyone cried out to God, *"Let him live! Live, live, live!"*

To our complete amazement, he began to come to. He suffered no broken bones, no cuts and no internal bleeding. He did have a bump on his head and sustained a slight concussion, but other than that he was fine.

Thank you Jesus!

About this time, I had been talking to my old buddy from college days, Sam, who was working with the youth at his church in New Orleans. We decided...well, mostly I decided - my poor wife had to endure my pride...that we should move to New Orleans and join him. So we did. We packed up and moved. The church gave us a sweet send-off and a baby shower as Patti was pregnant with our son Matthew Neil.

Our time in New Orleans was a mess. It didn't take long for me to realize how badly I had missed God. We decided to go back home to Illinois.

It never crossed my mind to call Capitol Hill and ask for my job back. I found out much later that the position remained open for a year after we left. All I had to do was call.

What a dummy.

But, let's face it, *stupid* is easy to do. All have sinned and fallen short of the glory of God.

Meanwhile, back in Illinois, after months of seeking employment and living with friends and family, God provided a position as manager of a clothing store.

From time to time I preached revivals on the weekends and eventually assumed the role of interim pastor with a small church in Potosi, Missouri.

Every Sunday and Wednesday we'd load up Sam and our newborn, Matthew, and drive almost two hours from Fairview Heights, Illinois to Potosi. The people there were so welcoming and we felt right at home with them. I was so comfortable that many times I would preach while holding Matthew in my arms.

It was during this time that I received a call about one of the young men from church that was hit in the face with a soft ball and suffered broken bones in his face. He was taken to Barnes Hospital in St. Louis where they were preparing him for surgery. I left at once, but it took me two hours to get there because of the traffic.

On the elevator ride up to his floor I felt the Holy Spirit tell me to anoint him with oil and he would be healed. Once I got to his room I discovered he hadn't gone into surgery yet because the x-ray machines were down. The family told me they had been praying for me to arrive before surgery.

"The Lord told me to anoint him with oil," I told them, "but I didn't bring any oil."

That's when I felt something odd in the palms of my hands. I raised them up to look at them and saw oil forming on my palms. I gently laid my hands on the young man's face, and he said he felt the bones move but was experiencing no pain.

An orderly arrived just as I finished praying, and took my young friend to the operating room. Within the hour the surgeon returned to the room with the young man.

"Will somebody please tell me what's going on here?" the doctor demanded. "He doesn't have any damage to his face."

There was no way to explain it, other than a miracle from God. We all rejoiced, and the doctor joined in.

✠✠✠

I was a guest on a radio show talking about how Jesus was the same yesterday, today and forever. As we talked about all the miracles we'd seen, a woman called in to the show claiming her daughter was in critical care dying of Hepatitis.

"Would you come pray for her?" the woman begged.

I went to the hospital where the girl was a patient. Her room was posted with a "No Visitors" sign, which I promptly ignored.

I walked into the room and sat down. I'd never seen anyone so yellow and frail. We talked about all the miracles described in the Bible and I asked if she believed them.

"Yes," she said.

"Do you believe all the words of the Bible are true?" I asked.

"Yes," she said.

"There is a verse that says, *Jesus is the same, yesterday, today and forever.* Do you believe that?" I asked.

I could see her faith rise as she nodded her head.

I prayed, cursed the disease and told her she would be home that weekend, for Thanksgiving dinner.

The one thing I didn't expect was the tongue-lashing I got from the girl's mother when I walked out of the room. The woman screamed coarse and vile words at me.

"How could you make such a promise to a dying girl?" she demanded.

I admit to being bemused by her attitude. After all, I thought that was why she had asked me to come and pray for her daughter.

The next week the woman called me to apologize and ask for my forgiveness. Her daughter's disease left the hour we had prayed. She went home the next day, completely healed.

✠✠✠

A pastor friend, whom I met through a college buddy of mine, invited me to conduct a revival at his Spirit-filled Southern Baptist church in Cahokia, Illinois. The meetings were scheduled to last for one week, but the Holy Spirit had other plans. Several weeks later it was still going strong as the Spirit continued to move in miraculous ways.

In one instance a mother brought her child who had been deaf from birth. I laid my hands on the little girl's ears and the first word she heard was the name of Jesus. The mother returned the next evening, testifying that the child was now repeating words she heard from her siblings at home.

I received a word of knowledge during that same service that God was going to heal someone who was dying from diabetes. Pastor Scott, raised his hand and declared, "I'm visiting a friend who is in the hospital. He has been told that if they don't amputate his leg tomorrow, the disease will kill him."

"I'll go with you to the hospital tomorrow, and we'll pray for him," I said.

I was not prepared for the awful sight at the hospital the next day. The man's leg was black from the knee down. Not just black, but...I'm not sure how else to describe it. He had a deep, nasty hole in his heel.

"The doctors are going to remove my leg today," he moaned as if resigned to his fate. "They say even if they take my leg, I might not survive the day."

"Perhaps, perhaps not," Pastor Scott replied, who then told him about the word of knowledge I had in church the day before. We prayed that not only would he live, but that his leg would be restored.

The doctors entered the room, examined the man's leg, consulted with each other, then decided to put off the surgery until the next day. For the next several days the scene was repeated. The doctors would gather to examine the man's leg, consult with each other and push back the procedure.

Each day the color of the man's leg changed progressively into a healthier pink, and by the end of the week looked perfectly well. The man's foot was another matter.

"We've saved your leg," the doctors told the man, taking credit for what I believed to be a divine work of the Holy Spirit, "but your foot still has that ugly wound. Even though it looks better, the best option might still be to amputate it. Whether we do or not, you will never walk on it again."

The man didn't say a word. Instead, he sat up on the edge of the bed, and then stood up and walked across the room.

"You must be in great pain," one doctor said.

"No," the man replied. "I have no pain at all."

Within another week the wound on the man's heel was gone. He was completely whole. Some might credit medical science, and I'm the first to say doctors can be the instrument of God's healing, but I'm equally convinced that earthly physicians could use a lot more help from the Master Physician. They would get it, too, if they'd ask. He's just like that.

Once the revival meeting came to an end, Pastor Scott's church offered me a position as assistant pastor. I told them the Lord was really speaking to Patti and me about returning to Jackson, Tennessee, where we attended Bible College. We felt like we were supposed to plant a church in that community, we just didn't know when. But I agreed to serve as assistant pastor until we knew it was time to leave.

Pastor Scott was the director of the local Metro East Baptist Association, and he felt I should be ordained back into the Southern Baptist denomination. Patti and I agreed, since we would once again be serving in a Southern Baptist church.

The ordination service ushered in a powerful encounter with the Holy Spirit. I approached the service with mixed emotions because it's easy for such an event to be all about the person being ordained. I never wanted there to be any glory coming my way, but always pointing toward Him. After all, the only true glory belongs to Him.

All of our family and friends were invited, and I had bought a new suit for the occasion.

The worship service was great, focused entirely on the Lord. Then it was time to "preach the charge" as they say. Pastor Scott, along with a couple of other local ministers, performed the formal rites, then asked Patti and I to come forward. They had placed a couple of chairs in the front where we were to sit as they prayed over us.

I admit to being a little embarrassed at being the center of all this attention.

We closed our eyes and they began to pray. It is traditional to anoint the head of ordination candidates with oil, so I wasn't too surprised when I felt warm oil pouring onto my head. I started to get a little concerned when the oil just kept flowing down over my head and long hair. At first I tried to keep it off my new suit, but I finally gave up.

Do they really have to ruin my new suit just to ordain me? I wondered.

Pastor Scott told Patti and me to stand. We stood up as he prayed this one last prayer over us. I don't know what happened next. It felt like a prize fighter socked hit me in the chin. I went down like a ton of bricks; out cold.

When I regained consciousness, I asked Patti what happened.

"Did he hit me?"

"No one even touched you," Patti answered. "Your head snapped back and you just fell down."

I just shook my head, bemused by it all.

"I'm still not real happy about Pastor Scott pouring that whole bottle of oil on my head and ruining my new suit," I muttered.

My friend, Ryan, just laughed and pointed at the pulpit. I looked, and there sat the bottle of anointing oil, still completely full.

"Feel your hair and your coat," Pastor Scott told me.

They were both dry. That's when it hit me; I had been anointed with the oil from heaven. I remained dumbfounded the rest of the night. What an amazing God we serve.

Chapter 7
Time To Go Forth

Over the next month, as Patti and I continued to pray about moving to Jackson, Tennessee, I asked the Lord for a confirmation. I had missed Him once. I didn't want to miss Him again.

The Holy Spirit spoke to me in prayer to call a pastor in St. Louis named David Crank, and that he would give me instructions on what I was to do.

I had never heard of this man, and wasn't sure he even existed, but in obedience called information in St. Louis for a phone number.

Sure enough, he was real.

I called on a Thursday night and his wife answered the phone. She told me I could find him at the Flaming Pit restaurant, where he conducted meetings every Thursday evening.

I shared this strange tale with a friend of mine, Ryan, an anointed worship leader.

"I know Pastor David," he said, to my surprise. "I've led worship for him. We should go to one of his Thursday night meetings and see what the Lord has in store for you."

I agreed, and the next Thursday we hit the road for St. Louis. Pastor David recognized Ryan immediately and invited him to minister in song before he shared the Word. I didn't get a chance to meet him before the service started, so I settled in to wait. I figured we'd have a chance to get to know each other after the service.

Pastor David spoke on how to know the voice of God and with such power I had never witnessed in a pastor before. As the service drew to its close he invited those who wanted prayer to come forward and stand across the front. I found myself on my feet and went to stand in line, although I wasn't really sure why I came forward.

I watched Pastor David as he ministered to the people. It was like he had read their mail. He just knew things about them. Some fell under the power of the Spirit, others didn't, but all received something.

When he came to me he just started laughing. His laughter got louder until he was roaring.

What is up with this guy? I wondered.

Then he pointed at me and said, "You are God's man for Jackson, Tennessee."

I'm sure my jaw hit the floor. He told me to stay after the service, that he had more of God's instructions to give me.

The next weekend Patti and I decided to go visit a church that we had close ties with from our youth pastoring days in Collinsville, Illinois. The church had a new pastor and we wanted to meet him. We sat in the center pew, about three rows back.

The new preacher was only a few minutes into his message when he stopped and looked right at us.

"Stand up," he said, pointing at us. "I can't go on until I give this word the Lord has placed on my heart. The Lord keeps saying, 'You're the man for Jackson, Tennessee.' Does this mean something to you?"

"Yes, sir, it does," we replied, "very much so."

We now had total confidence we were hearing from God again, but we still wanted to do things decently and in order. I went to Pastor Scott and prayed with him for a few weeks more about our decision to move to Tennessee. Once we all had peace about it, we set a date for the move, but we still needed a place to stay and money to make the trip on.

A couple in the church offered us the use of their travel trailer until we had a place to stay in Jackson. The church took up a special offering, the total sum of two hundred dollars, a generous amount in those days, and we were ready to go.

We stored our furniture and headed off on this new and exciting adventure. We found a campground in Jackson to set up the travel trailer, then went to work establishing our new ministry in town. The conference hall on the sixth floor of a local bank was offered to us for Thursday night meetings, and the local newspaper offered to run a feature story about our new work in the city.

A lady in town, Ann Twyford, read that newspaper article and sent us a message at the campground's phone number (we didn't have cell phones in those days). When I returned her call, she invited us to meet with her and some friends so we could share our vision for the new ministry.

After the meeting ended, these precious ladies declared that this was the kind of church they had been praying for the Lord to bring to Jackson. They gave us a spontaneous offering of eighty dollars. It was another example of God's daily provision in our lives.

When the night of our first Thursday night meeting arrived, Pastor Scott came down and brought us another offering of eighty dollars. The offering from the first night was eighty dollars, too.

What is the significance of these first three eighty dollar gifts? Three represents the Trinity and the number eight in scripture often represents new beginnings. This just shows how intricately God is involved as He orders our steps.

That was the beginning of an eight year run as pastor of what would become Word of Life Christian Outreach Center.

We soon outgrew the bank's conference room and moved our meetings to a VFW hall. The offerings increased to the point that we could finally start looking for an apartment. Again, God used Miss Ann as she took a step of faith and offered us one side of her duplex. She believed God would provide our rent to her each month. He did just that. We never missed a payment.

I had found a very nice, but vacant, business complex on the edge of town and asked the owner if we could rent it. I asked for the first three months rent free, then the next six months at half rent.

"I'll have to ponder that," he replied.

The next Sunday our tiny, but growing, congregation met at that business complex. We had a sound system in place and the chairs set up. We had a great service and continued to meet there for several years.

The people in the area really wanted the church to be there. The congregation continued to grow and to keep up we had to rent the whole complex just to have enough classrooms. Members bought chairs for their family and another for a visitor. Many great times were shared in our services as we gathered each week.

During our first year in this complex the families in our church asked us to start a Christian School. We launched with kindergarten through twelfth grade. The Lord also blessed us greatly when a wonderful couple from back home came to help us in our work. He was an excellent teacher of the Word, and since he had retired from civil service he was able to pastor without pay.

The church wasn't the only thing that was growing. By this time Patti was expecting our fourth child, and we were out-growing our cozy little duplex. We decided we were ready to move into our own house.

I took my associate pastor along on a house-hunting excursion, and found one on the golf course that I fell in love with. It was beautiful. The house had a full basement with a two car garage and a wooded lot. It was also way above our pay grade, but as I walked around it the Lord spoke to me; *This is your house.*

I went by the real estate agent's office and made an offer on the house.

"I'll pay $60,000 but the seller will have to give me six months to secure the loan. I can't pay more than $600 per month until we close and that amount will have to represent my down payment at closing."

"The house lists for $120,000 and I've never heard of such an offer before," she replied. "And you'll have to put up some kind of down payment for me to take the offer to the seller."

I turned to my associate pastor.

"Can I borrow a dollar until tomorrow?" I asked.

He pulled a dollar out of his wallet and I handed it to the real estate agent. She thought I was kidding. I wasn't.

"This is the most bizarre deal I've ever handled," she sighed. But she took the dollar and made the offer.

The seller didn't even make a counter-offer. He accepted the deal right away. Within six months we had our financing in place and closed on our home. We enjoyed living in that house in the woods for a couple of years. Not that the golf course was that big a deal to me. I didn't play.

✠✠✠

Our home on the golf course, purchased for $1 down.

"Did you get paid this week," Patti asked me one Monday morning.

That might sound like an odd question to you, but it wasn't uncommon for us to give our weekly paycheck away to someone who needed it more than we did.

"Yes," I replied, "but I gave it away this morning. Why?"

Patti obviously upset. She took me into the kitchen and opened the cupboards and refrigerator.

"That's why," she said.

We were pretty much down to nothing in the house to eat.

"Make a grocery list of the things we need and we'll pray over it," I said. "Somehow God will supply."

Patti's list was two pages long. We prayed, then went about our daily business.

A few hours later we heard a knock at the door. Joanne from church was there. She and her husband owned the local Piggly Wiggly grocery store.

"What brings you to our neck of the woods?" I asked as I opened the door and invited her in.

"Pastor Don," she replied, "I hope you are not offended, but I have been thinking about Sunday's message on *How to Know the Voice of God*. I went to the store this morning to buy a few things, and I thought the Lord told me to get you guys some groceries. My trunk is full. Can I bring them in?"

I helped her bring the bags into the house, and when we unloaded we found everything that was on Patti's list. It was even the name brand stuff that we usually couldn't afford.

We had a celebration because God had met our need and were excited for Joanne because He had taught her how to hear His voice.

✠✠✠

The Lord blessed us with our fourth child, Caroline Elise, while we lived in that home. We planned a home birth, using midwives from Memphis and traveled the hour and a half there and back for exams and birthing classes.

It was during one of those visits in Memphis that we had a divine meeting with Dr. Brown and his wife, Sandy, who were also from Jackson and expecting their second child. They soon became good friends and a part of our church family. Steve served as our family doctor for many years.

It was a God-connection, and I mention it because it shows how easily we can overlook our heavenly Father's work in our lives. Simple encounters that we might consider coincidences, are actually God ordained. I think it is profitable for us to think about moments like these, rather than solely focusing on great healings and big miracles.

God sent this family to our church to be a part of His healing ministry. The community learned of God's use of home births as the local newspaper featured a full-page article about our families' births, complete with color pictures of our newborn Carli. God took center stage as the article highlighted natural childbirth methods that have been around long before modern methods.

We are not opposed to modern delivery techniques. We have done them all; hospital, birthing rooms and home delivery. I believe they are all acceptable in the eyes of God. We just prefer the old-fashion way, if at all possible.

Carli is our only daughter among four brothers, since her sister lives in heaven. I call her *Sissie*. She is our rose.

✠✠✠

Patti and I wanted to build a log home. We went looking for land to build on, and found it out in the country near the small community of Humboldt, Tennessee. The beautiful hilltop looked like *Little House on The Prairie* to us. The land was owned by a little elderly lady, and it wasn't on the market, but after a couple of visits she agreed to sell it to us.

An old-fashioned barn raising for our Log Home in Humboldt, Tennessee.

Soon after we bought the land, we read an article in the local newspaper about a woman who had won a Coca-Cola giveaway. The grand prize was a log home, which she had no use for. She put the prize up for sale for $12,000.

We called her, met with her, and agreed to buy the log home from her...for $6,000. The catch was, the prize was for all the components of the log home, but you had to put it together yourself.

We had land, we had the logs, and fortunately we had the folks at church who were willing to help out with an old fashioned barn-raising. We arranged for the log company to set the logs, and our group did all the finish work.

We sold our little house in the big woods, and now had our little house on the prairie - all for a sum total of $63,000. But that was not our last real estate deal.

We had outgrown our meeting facilities and needed a larger church building. I went on the hunt again.

Just outside of town was a burned out metal building that had once housed The Golden Circle Club, a notorious night club with a bad reputation. I still don't know the whole story, whether the fire was accidental or intentional. All I know for sure is that it burned and was now for sale.

The property included four acres, two of which were paved. As I walked across the property I could feel the Spirit of the Lord all over this place. When I got back home, I told Patti about the property and we prayed for the right price to offer for it.

I received the answer to our prayers while shaving the next morning. Our young son, Matthew, came in with a calculator in hand and showed me the numbers he had punched in; 77,777. I figured he had just pushed down the number seven and held it, but I knew this was the number from the Lord.

I called the real estate agent who handled the property and said I wanted to put in an offer. We met at her office where she told me the asking price was $250,000.

I just smiled. I knew this was our building.

"I'd like to offer $77,777."

"He'll never go for it," she shook her head. "I know this guy. He's a hard negotiator."

"I'd like for you to take the offer to him anyway," I said.

She sighed and said she would.

The property owner countered with $200,000.

"It's a good counter," the real estate agent said. "You'd be crazy not to take it."

"I don't think so," I said. "Tell him we'll give him $77,777."

She came back and said he would consider an offer of $150,000.

"Tell him I'm not playing a game with him," I said. "Tell him $77,777 is the amount the Lord told me to buy that property for, and that's all we are willing to spend."

Meanwhile the folks in our congregation were getting antsy. They wanted to know how the negotiations were going.

"We'll get the property," I said. "Just believe."

A couple of weeks went by before we heard from the real estate agent again. She finally called and said, "Okay, he said he'll take $77,777."

"That's great," I replied, "but here is the rest of the offer. The property is going to take extensive renovation. We'll need around $20,000 for that. Tell him we want him to go to the bank and borrow $100,000 for us. That will be enough to cover the cost of the property, the renovations and your commission."

"I'll take him your offer," she sighed once again, "but there is not a snowball's chance that he'll take it."

A couple of hours later she called me back.

"He said he'll do it," she told me. "He said he hasn't had a night's rest since starting to deal with you and just wants to get some sleep."

Working on the remodel of that building was one of the best times of my life. My father-in-law is an electrician and he came down to wire the building. But it turned into more than just a wonderful father-in-law and son moment. We had a God encounter while working on that building.

It happened at the end of a long day of wiring. We stood at the back doors and surveyed the day's work before leaving. The doors were locked and we had our back to them facing the electrical closet in front of us.

As we stooped down to gather our tools, we sensed someone behind us. We both turned around and there were two young men who looked to be in their 20's, just standing there, staring at us.

"Can I help you?" I asked.

"No," one of the young men replied. "We're on a pilgrimage for the Lord, and were told to stop and see the man building the church."

The other said, "This used to be Satan's house. Now it's the house of the glory of the Lord."

Goose bumps sprouted all over me. Those were the very words I had used to describe this building to our congregation the Sunday before.

"Would you like to help us work on this building?" I asked.

"We *could* do that," the first young man answered. "But we have others to see."

They asked if I knew the pastor at the First Assembly of God.

"Yes," I said. "He is a blessed brother."

"You have answered rightly," the second young man said. "We were told to bring you this tithe."

He pulled out a perfect square of money. I had never seen money folded like that before. From the look on my father-in-law's face, he hadn't either.

I took the money-square, thanked them and slipped it in my pocket. They then asked if we would bless them so they could be on their way. After I prayed for them we turned to gather our tools. By the time we turned back around they were gone.

We stood there for a few moments, dumbfounded. We checked the back doors. They were locked. We ran to the front door. No one was there either. The parking lot was empty.

"Let's take one more look through the building," my father-in-law suggested. We did, but we found no one.

I told my father- in -law those were angels. He was unbelieving and very perplexed at where they could have gone. A few weeks later, he told the story to a visiting missionary at his church back home.

The missionary just laughed and said, "Bob, those weren't young men, those were angels."

The Bible says that some people have entertained angels unaware. We were sure aware of those two.

Burned out remains of the former Golden Circle Club.

Chapter 8
Favor With God And Man

We found favor with the Southern Baptist Convention, once again, as I was now an ordained SBC pastor. We also had a great relationship with the Assemblies of God, J.R. Gould, (the pastor the angel referred to and who later served as Tennessee's Superintendent) and many other pastors of non-denominational churches.

Starting a pastors' softball team united us in friendship and common purpose. Joint revivals and shared service projects helped to further the cause of Christ in our communities and bind us together even more strongly.

One Sunday the Lord healed a little girl from deafness in much the same fashion as the healing in Pastor Scott's church back in Illinois. On this occasion I was ministering during a special revival at our church. The Lord spoke to me that there was a young deaf child present, and God wanted to heal her. A woman who was not a member of our congregation brought her granddaughter forward. The Lord opened her ears and we all rejoiced as it became apparent that she was hearing. Later that evening the woman returned and testified that the child was mimicking sounds made by her older siblings.

Today, our son, Matt, calls those kind of experiences, *old school.* Our *God is the same yesterday, today and forever.*

Not all of our spiritual encounters involved healing. In fact, one of my favorite encounters was of a completely different category.

Patti was leading us into the presence of the Lord. We only had a piano and guitar in the room, but as Patti played everyone heard other instruments accompanying her worship.

On another occasion when she was leading us into worship I saw a silhouette of the Lord enter the room. His presence was so strong I jumped down off the platform and pressed my face on the ground. Patti kept her eyes closed and people were falling over in their seats and joining me kneeling on the floor.

The only way to describe that experience was awe-some (and I don't mean in the flippant way that word is commonly used; I mean we were all filled with awe!). That wife of mine sure knows how to get into His presence in worship. I believe every follower of Christ can have that intimate kind of worship experience with God. He will show up if invited properly, at least, that's my take on it.

✠✠✠

During our childbearing days ultrasounds were just beginning to be used and usually only if complications were suspected. We never knew whether we were going to have a boy or a girl, but one thing we were certain of, our babies loved worship services, even in the womb. When Patti became pregnant with our next child, the baby would kick, roll around and just carry on as her guitar rested against her belly.

A prophet, Bobby Hernandez from Oklahoma, stayed with us for a week, and one night he had a word for Patti and me.

We don't remember word for word, but we'll never forget two main things he stated. He said that this child would be used as a leader in praise and worship and that he would be a mighty warrior in worship.

We noticed that Bobby said "he" would be a mighty warrior. We kind of laughed about it and said that this must be a boy.

Bobby then stepped out of the room to make a call home. He said he wanted to tell his wife about what the Lord was doing in the meetings here. When he returned to the living room he handed us a check for five hundred dollars.

"My wife and I want to be the first to sow into your baby's ministry," he said. "Use this for his birth."

We did, and as if you might guess, the baby was a boy. We named him Dallas Joseph, and even as a young child he loved banging on plastic bowls, the furniture, the walls and anything else that made noise. We thought it best to buy a drum set for him. Now many drum sets later, he helps lead worship unto the Lord and is a mighty warrior for the kingdom of God.

When Dallas was nine months old, Patti would let Matt carry him downstairs from his crib. She sensed a check in her spirit each time and thought, "He's too young to do that." Because she was feeling tired one day, she went against the prompting and sent Matt upstairs to bring Dallas down. About 5 steps from the bottom, he slipped on the step, sending Dallas head first to the wooden floor.

Patti called me at the office. She was beside herself with fear.

"Just pray and hold him," I told her. "I will be right there."

All the way home I prayed and cursed the spirit of death. I was still praying in the Spirit as I walked through the door of our home.

I took Dallas in my arms, holding his swollen head firm against my chest. He was screaming, but I prayed louder, crying out against the powers of darkness. I reminded God that this child was His worshiper. I declared that no weapon formed against him would prosper.

As I continued to wage war in the heavenly, little by little, Dallas settled down. We took him to the doctor and though his head was swollen on the side, he was fine. God gave us the victory.

Jeremiah 1:12 says God watches over His word to perform it. God heard my words, His words and performed it. Glory to God! When fear comes in, the Word kicks in and casts fear out. The Word of God brings perfect peace.

✠✠✠

My good friend Tyo Lancaster was an elder at his church. He was hungry for the power of God in his life, and we would get together from time to time just to brag on God. On one occasion when we were together, he wanted to visit a middle aged woman who was ill and pray for her. Since I didn't know the woman and was unfamiliar with her illness, I told him I would just wait in the car.

He went inside, and I prayed while sitting in the car, but after a few moments he came back out and motioned for me to join him. As I walked through the door Tyo said, "This is a pastor friend of mine." The first words out of my mouth to her were, "You have cancer of the lymph nodes."

The woman gave me a bemused look, then nodded and quietly acknowledged, "I do have cancer of the lymph nodes."

Tyo looked at me with pursed lips.

"I didn't tell you that," he said. "How did you know?"

I just looked at him. He knew how I knew.

We laid hands on the woman and prayed for her complete healing. On her next visit to the doctor, they found no more cancer.

In addition to pastoring I hosted a radio program that reached from Tennessee, up into Missouri and across into Arkansas. We recorded the program at the radio station, but it was broadcast later, and when listeners called in, the calls were routed to my office at the church.

A woman called me about her son who was a patient at a military hospital in St. Louis. She asked if I would go and see him.

I agreed to go.

When I arrived at the hospital they told me the young man was dying of a disease. I walked in his room before they could tell me to keep out.

"God will heal you today if you will repent from your sin," I told him, then I named the sin he had kept hidden from the world.

"Who told you about this," the young man sputtered. "Nobody knows about this, not even my mother."

"Your Father in heaven knows," I replied. "He sent me, and He told me that if you will repent, ask

God to forgive and receive His Son as your savior, you will be healed."

The young man obviously knew a good deal when he saw one. He prayed right then.

I got a call from his mother a couple weeks later. She said her son was home and that he was completely healed.

The Word says that if we confess our sins He is faithful to forgive us our sins and cleanse us from all unrighteousness. That is what He did, and that is what He is still doing. He is the same yesterday, today and forever.

✠✠✠

The 700 Club got a call from a man in a nearby town who was contemplating suicide. They called me to see if I could meet with him. He lived in a rough area, but I hurried over anyway.

There was no answer when I knocked on his door. I knocked again but still got no response. As I turned to walk away I noticed fresh blood on the steps leading into the house. As I studied the blood the door opened. There stood a man with a rag around his hand.

"Are you the man from the 700 Club?" he asked.

"I am," I replied.

"Please come in," he said.

I had a bad feeling about it, but I followed the man as he led me through this dark house to the backroom. We sat down. The 700 Club was still on the television. He turned the volume down.

"What's wrong?" I asked.

A loud, evil voice spoke from the man, but I knew it wasn't his voice.

"I am going to kill you and I am going to kill him."

"No," I shouted right back. "You will not kill anyone, because the One who is in me is greater than you. Tell me your name!"

"I don't have a name," the foul spirit replied.

"Yes you do," I countered. "The Holy Spirit will give me your name."

I called out the name the Holy Spirit whispered to me and commanded the demon to go. The man slumped forward, then he raised his eyes to meet mine. I could see there were more demons in him. I called out another name, and another name. After casting out more than a half-dozen demons I was starting to get exhausted, but the Holy Spirit strengthened me.

I would call the demons to come out, and the voice would answer, "There are no more demons here." It would have been funny except that a man's life was at stake. I had to be sure this house was clean before I left.

The last demon refused to go.

"You don't know me," it proclaimed, "and you can't make me go."

"I may not know you, but I know the One who does know you, and He is greater than you," I reminded him.

Demons hate the Word of God. It is like setting a match to them. The man jumped up and tried to back away from me. I grabbed him by the arm and swung him around to face me. His eyes glazed over and he growled at me like a wild animal.

"I won't go," it snarled. "You don't know my name. I will kill this man!"

That's when the Lord revealed its name to me.

"Your name is suicide," I said.

"No," it whimpered. "That's not my name."

"Yes, it is," I said. "In the name of Jesus I command you to go."

The man bent forward, vomited, and fell to the floor as if he were dead. A moment later his hands grabbed my leg and he looked up at me. His eyes were completely clear.

"Thank you, Jesus," he whispered.

That's when I realized He didn't see me at all. All he could see was Jesus. After he regained his senses, the man asked me what happened.

"You might want to sit down and get comfortable," I said. "This is going to take a while."

"What happened to your hand?" I asked him.

He pointed to a brand new pocket knife on the table. Two of its blades were broken off and lying to the side.

"I was watching the 700 Club," he explained, when a voice inside my head said, *kill yourself.* I took out my new knife put it to my wrist, but when I pulled it across my wrist the blade fell off. I pulled out the second blade and put it to my wrist. That blade fell off, too. That's when Ben on the 700 Club said, *don't kill yourself. Right now pick up the phone and call us, we can help*. So I did. They told me someone would come right away to see me."

"What do you do for a living?" I asked.

"I'm the worship leader at our church," he replied.

I couldn't believe what I was hearing. A Christian with demons? How could this be?

After talking for a long time he admitted that he had gotten involved with witchcraft. It started out with what he thought was an innocent fascination with Ouija boards, then Tarot cards, then progressed into groups speaking to the dead. He had surrendered his lordship over to the dark side.

Remember the verse that says Satan is like a roaring lion going about seeking whom he may devour? Don't be deceived into thinking you are immune to the attacks of the devil. Stay in the Word of God, pray without ceasing and fellowship with those of like faith.

✠✠✠

Howard Ellison, our sound man at church, was moving. He asked me if Tommy, my associated pastor, and I could come over and help out.

When we arrived, Howard's dad was already there. A former constable, he was one of the biggest men I had ever met. When I started to walk through the door, Mr. Ellison came through from the other direction and completely blocked the door.

He stopped me, poked his finger into my chest and said, none to kindly, "I am a Baptist. My son is a Baptist. We are always going to be Baptist."

It appeared to me that he wanted to pick a fight.

"That's great," I responded with a smile. "I'm a Baptist, too!"

I'm not sure what he had planned to say next, but whatever it was fell to the wayside. Instead, he changed the subject.

"You will never guess what I have in my pocket, preacher," the big man said.

"You have a miniature anvil in your pocket," I said.

You could see his eyes go wide as he reached into the pocket of his bib overalls and pulled out a miniature anvil. Mr. Ellison didn't say another word to me. He quietly went outside to see his son. They conversed for a few moments, then he left.

Howard walked over to me and said, "My dad wanted to know how you knew what he had in his pocket. I told him, 'Dad, the Lord talks to that man. He knows if you've got cancer or some other kind of disease in your body.'"

A few months later we heard that Mr. Ellison had a serious stroke. I was asked to go to the hospital and pray for him. When I got there Mr. Ellison was lying on his side facing the window.

"He hasn't opened his eyes or moved a muscle since he got here," his attending nurse told me.

"Mr. Ellison," I said, "It's the preacher that knew you had an anvil in your pocket."

When he heard that he rolled over toward me and opened his eyes. He didn't speak, but he was awake. The nurse's jaw hit the floor.

I talked to Mr. Ellison for a long while. I knew he had a strong relationship with the Lord, but I told him we would all like for him to choose to stay and not leave. I guess he got a better offer to leave, because I was one of the last to see him awake.

I was asked to preside at his funeral. He was a well-known and beloved member of his community, and there was not enough room in the funeral home for all the people who came to pay their respects. The family gave the miniature anvil to me, and I used it in my message.

"Mr. Ellison loved the Lord Jesus," I told the assembled mourners. "I know he would want to take this last opportunity to witness his love for Christ and I know he would love to see all of you in heaven where he has gone."

It's not a common practice to give an invitation at a funeral, but the presence of the Lord was so strong that I felt encouraged to do so. In this case it was the right thing to do. The house was full of tears, not because Mr. Ellison was gone, but because the presence of the Lord in that place was so powerful.

✠✠✠

There was one thing missing that would make our log home complete - a porch swing.

Patti specifically wanted a contoured porch swing made of oak. She wanted the long version so she and the kids could all swing together. One Friday as I was praying, I asked the Lord to provide it.

"Lord," I prayed, "my wife is the sweetest and best gift you have ever given me. You know she doesn't ask for much. Would you please give her an oak porch swing that is contoured?"

We had learned years before from listening to Dr. Paul Cho, who pastors in South Korea, to be specific in our prayers. I wanted to make sure I prayed for the exact kind of porch swing that would bless my wife. I didn't tell a soul about the swing or the prayer.

Two days later, as we all had just walked onto our front porch and entered our home after church, Carli said, "Daddy, I want to go on the swing."

"Sure honey," I told her. "We'll leave early for the evening church service so you can play on the swings at church."

"No Daddy," Carli said even more determinately, "I want to go on the swing."

I tried to reason with her again but she would not be stopped and took my hand pulling me back outside to the porch. Sure enough when we walked out onto the porch, there was a long oak, contoured porch swing with chains to hang it by, just sitting there. It had cobwebs on it, as if it had been stored away in someone's barn. To this day we don't know who brought it, but someone was sure listening to His voice.

It just goes to show that God is interested in things that encourage and bring joy to his kids. Those were tough financial times for us, but He always provided our needs, and He even gave us *the icing on the cake.*

Carli on the porch of the Log Home.

Chapter 9
A New Door

God has often used our ministry as something of a bridge; a connecting point between people, causes and ministries. On at least two occasions while we were in Jackson, the Lord sent pastors to me who were seeking a word of confirmation regarding their future ministry.

On one occasion a man I didn't know knocked on my office door and asked to come in. He introduced himself as a pastor from Kentucky. He had just resigned the position at his church, and told me was looking for direction.

"The Lord spoke to me to find His apostle, Don McCain in Jackson, Tennessee," he said. "The Lord told me you would have a word for me."

Then he just sat there, expectantly.

I confess to being taken a bit off-guard. The Lord certainly hadn't talked to me about this guy and I didn't know what he needed. But I knew he had driven several hours to see me, and I didn't want to miss the Lord in this dealing.

"Let's go to lunch," I invited, "and we can talk about it."

We visited for a couple hours. I honestly don't remember what I said, but it obviously resonated in that man's spirit.

"That's it!" he declared. "That's the word that I came for."

He thanked me, then went on his way. I never saw him again.

I had a similar experience a few weeks later. Another pastor traveled several hours and showed up unannounced at my office door. Once again we went to lunch, I said something that was confirmed in his spirit, and that man went off and started a successful new church.

Both of these men had left their former positions as pastors because they had received the baptism of the Holy Spirit as evidenced by speaking in tongues, which was not acceptable in their respective denominations.

Perhaps I said something like, *You have to answer to the one who called you, not the denomination or people to whom you minister.*

What is good for the goose is good for the gander, as the old saying goes. While my situation was really nothing like the ones facing those two brothers, since the congregation I pastored was accustomed to the moving of the Holy Spirit, God is in the business of opening and closing doors. It's our job to respond to those opening and closing doors, and I sensed in my spirit that the Lord was about to move us to a different place.

Our lives belong to Him and whatever He wants us to do is what we must do. But my own words applied to me as well as to those walking through difficult and unpleasant circumstances: *We are not called to please men, but to please God.*

I have been a missionary, youth pastor, senior pastor, evangelist, prophet, apostle, deacon and elder and have worked in secular work. Whatever title you want to put on your job, we are all in fulltime ministry. There are no big shots or no little shots in the kingdom of heaven. There are only brothers and sisters of the same Father in heaven, all called to live daily, walking by faith and obeying His voice.

"I need to sleep downstairs on the couch tonight," I told Patti. "I sense the Lord wants to speak to me in the night."

He did.

The next morning I told Patti I needed to drive to Nashville, Tennessee. The Lord told me our gifts were needed there, and I needed to discover what God was calling us to do.

I left that morning and spent the whole day driving from one end of town to the other; from Hendersonville in the north to Franklin in the south.

While I was in Hendersonville I drove past an empty church building. The Lord spoke to me to lay hands on it and prophecy over it. (Please don't get the idea that prophecy is some weird, spooky phenomenon. To prophesy means to speak to something; to call it to be something it is not).

God didn't tell me to start a church there, but simply to speak over that building, that it would come back to life and be the house of the Lord it was originally intended to be.

Within a few years that building became the ministry center for Paul Crouch's TBN Ministries in Tennessee.

I drove south until I came across The Lord's Chapel on Nolensville Road. Once again I felt the urging of the Holy Spirit to pray over that facility. I pulled into the parking lot, walked into the office and asked if I could speak to the pastor.

"We don't currently have a pastor," the secretary told me. "We do have a youth pastor. You can speak with him, if you like."

I introduced myself to the young man and explained why I was in town. He allowed me to pray over the facility, and when I was finished he said, "I believe you are supposed to be our next pastor."

I just smiled.

"You might be right," I told him. "But it's not likely."

He told the church board about me, but they eventually called an evangelist, who was a friend of mine, to be their pastor.

I left The Lord's Chapel and drove farther south through the tiny community of Nolensville. It felt like home, and I got the impression we were supposed to move to that town.

I proceeded on down to Franklin. When I got there, the Lord spoke to me about holding meetings in a downtown bank. I said, "Yes, sir," then turned around and drove back to Jackson to tell Patti everything that had transpired during the short span of 24 hours.

We packed up and moved to Nolensville Tennessee. We found the perfect house in one day, rented it and moved in before the week was over. It was a good thing, too, because we had sold our home in Jackson, and the people who bought it needed to move in immediately.

As we loaded up the U-Haul through the front door the new owners unloaded their moving van through the back door.

It worked out great for both families, and just proved to me once again that when the Lord closes one door, He always opens another.

We started holding meetings in that Franklin bank as soon as we settled into our new home in Nolensville. Neither Patti nor I felt like we were there to plant a new church. Instead, I had a strong urging from the Spirit that I was to shepherd this small group of families.

I got a couple of regular jobs so we could eat and pay our bills. One of the families in the group opened their home for meetings, so we moved out of the bank building. We loved this small group, and the power of the Lord was awesome and evident when we met together.

Gathering together in prayer and waiting for the Lord to move was always something we would do together. Sometimes Sharon McCormick, who owned the home where we met, would get impressions in her spirit. I loved to hear her prophesy, because she had such a humble spirit. Whenever she said, "I see..." it was always good.

On one occasion we had a visitor in our midst. When Sharon started to prophesy, you could see on the visitor's face that she was not too sure about this whole thing.

I had an impression from the Lord and shared it the same way Sharon had been doing.

"I see a wagon being pulled that is full of gifts," I said. The gifts are wrapped and need to be opened."

The woman started laughing loudly.

I was surprised by her outburst and stopped prophesying.

"What is going on in your spirit," I asked.

I had not met the woman prior to the start of the meeting didn't even know her name. It was obvious that she had been raised in the traditions of the old South. She just exuded that Southern Lady vibe. If you've ever spent much time in the South, you know what I mean.

"Mr. McCain," she said formally. "My name is Miss Wagoner and I came here tonight to find out about the gifts of the Holy Spirit."

Once again God was using us as bridge makers. We were there that night to bring Miss Wagoner from where she was, over to where she needed to be for the next portion of her spiritual journey.

That was the case for most of the people in this small group. In the not-too-distant future many were called to different parts of the country. We weren't there to plant a church. Instead God was using us to bridge the gap and impart what those folks would need as they continued to serve the Lord in their new environments.

Some women from Smyrna, Tennessee, a small town about 20 minutes southeast of Nashville, attended those meetings. One night they shared that a pastor they knew was going through a divorce and needed prayer.

"Will you go and see him," they asked.

I agreed, and met the man. Although he cared greatly for his congregation, I realized he needed to get his own life straightened out before he could effectively lead. He asked if I would take care of his congregation.

Patti and I agreed, although we truly had neither the calling nor desire to pastor this church. A new family began coming to the church, and the husband had recently graduated from Rhema Bible College. He had a great desire to shepherd this flock, and we were happy to turn this group over to him as pastor. Once again we were used as a bridge.

Everyone needs a church to call home and we were no exception. We felt called to The Lord's

Chapel and settled in there for the next two years. I volunteered to serve in whatever capacity they needed, while holding down two secular jobs. I managed a men's clothing store and worked construction, while Patti continued to homeschool our children.

It was during this time that I met Dwight Marable, the director of Missions International. Dwight facilitated missions work all around the world. He was planning a ten-day crusade for Romania, and felt that I was the right evangelist to conduct those meetings. I felt the Lord say, "Go," so I agreed.

I was in a prayer group with NASCAR legend Darrell Waltrip that met each Tuesday morning. Those men were prayer warriors. When I told them about the upcoming mission trip, they covenanted to cover my venture in prayer. They were the real deal, and I felt their support throughout that trip.

Chapter 10
God Is Real Big

Dwight had met Doru Pop, a pastor who had been exiled by the former Romanian government for practicing Christianity. When the old government collapsed, Pastor Doru saw an opportunity to return to his homeland and revitalize its churches. That's where our little missionary group entered the picture.

Our group was 16 members strong when we set out for Romania. This was 1991, shortly after the fall of the Berlin Wall, and we were among the first Western missionaries to enter this Communist country.

The first leg of our journey took us to the Netherlands where we changed planes for the flight into Munich, Germany. From there we boarded rented Volkswagen vans and embarked on an extended road trip across Germany, Austria and Hungary. The journey was long and it was exhausting, but it was also exhilarating.

The family sending Don off to Romania.

I couldn't help but ponder how preposterous it was that God had opened the doors for a country farm boy like me to travel the world. We saw the great cities of Europe, the amazing architecture of Budapest, Hungary, the majestic Austrian Alps, and the hills of Salzburg, where The Sound of Music was filmed. It was the trip of a life time.

Of course, our group got lost.

Two extra hours were spent looking for the border crossing from Hungary into Romania. We were tired, more than a little frustrated and our patience was wearing thin. As Americans we tend to want things done our way, on our time-table.

One thing I've learned over the years - God is not particularly concerned with *our* way or *our* time-table. He has His own way and His own time-table and he expects us to be concerned with it.

Eventually the border crossing came into sight. We drove up behind a line of vehicles and waited our turn. That's when I noticed something was not right in the small car in front of us. The driver started thrashing around violently enough to cause the car to rock back and forth.

Dr. Tad Porter, a physician from Nashville was a member of our party. He didn't hesitate for a moment.

"Let's go," he called out, and we all jumped out of the van and ran to the car.

Tad jerked open the driver's door. By this time the man was not breathing and was blue in the face. He pulled the man out of the car and laid him on the ground.

Tad administered emergency CPR, while another member of our party ran for the border guard to ask him to call an ambulance. The rest of us prayed.

Tad worked on the unconscious man for the next twenty minutes while we waited for help to come, but to no avail. The man died.

"I've done all I can do," said a completely exhausted Dr. Tad. "His heart has burst. I can't do any more."

Tad gave me a look that said, *help*.

I don't remember even thinking about it. I cried out loud, "In the name of Jesus, arise!"

The man sat up straight with such force that he tossed Tad aside. The crowd that had gathered, including the border guards, were astonished as you can imagine.

"I am sore amazed," I said. I felt like one of the first century disciple who had just watched Jesus perform a miracle.

Dr. Porter made the man sit still for an examination.

"I can't find anything wrong with him," he said.

The paramedics, who had finally arrived, did their own examination and couldn't find anything wrong with the man either.

The man didn't have a clue what had just happened to him. His wife, who had been silent in fear through it all, was now weeping, overwhelmed with great joy.

We had no trouble out of those border guards. They passed us straight through into Romania.

God raising someone from the dead? What a way to start a mission trip! And to think, if we had our way, we would have missed that miracle by two hours.

Don with local children in Romania.

✠✠✠

We eventually arrived at Doru's family home. I stayed with Doru and his wife in their apartment. The rest of the group stayed with other family members.

While much had been done in preparation for our visit, there was still much to do. Dwight, Dr. Porter, Doru and a few others went into the town of Targu Mures to make final arrangements for the upcoming meetings.

The KGB was still very much active in the region, and they did not *get a witness* on our mission, as we say in the South. They detained our party and interrogated them about our visit. The local magistrate was furious. He cancelled our use of the coliseum, and denied us access to the national radio to advertise the event.

"You have come to turn our cities upside down," he accused.

Our team members said nothing. They quietly waited for the Spirit of the Lord to move on our behalf.

"Go," the magistrate finally said. "And when your visas expire, you had better be gone."

The team returned home where the rest of us waited and told us the bad news.

"I know a pastor in town," Doru said. "Let me give him a call. Perhaps he can help."

Within the hour we were set for our first meeting in a small church on the outskirts of town. We spent the remainder of the day praying and preparing ourselves for the outpouring of God that we expected during the meeting.

The small church building was designed to hold around 100 people. When we arrived, there were twice that many people eager to get in. The pastor said it was the largest crowd the church had ever seen.

The word spread about our meetings like wildfire, and people walked for miles to come. And of course the Holy Spirit showed up, too. There were numerous salvations and a number of healings. These people had lived under atheistic communism for a generation. They had never witnessed words of knowledge before or seen people instantaneously healed.

As word spread about the moving of the Holy Spirit, we received invitations to come and minister throughout the region. We were soon booked for every night of our trip. Each night we were in a different village, in increasingly larger facilities, which were always packed out. The crowds grew so large that at times there were more people outside the facility than inside. The locals simply opened the windows so those on the outside could experience what was happening inside.

One night I had to walk across the tops of the pews to make it from the back of the church to the front. I was humbled by the obvious hunger for God in those meetings.

"Lord, why isn't it this way in America?" I wondered.

The Lord revealed to me that persecution drives people to desire freedom from tyranny. The people of Romania had been in bondage for decades. Americans are in bondage too, just of a different kind. Once America discovers that it is living under tyranny without Christ, I believe we'll see revival break out and multitudes will flock to Him.

Governments rise and fall. The bondage they place on their citizens is temporal, because those governments are temporal. Our eternal citizenship is in a kingdom that is not of this world. The kingdom of

Heaven brings true freedom, true liberty, and it will never come to an end.

On Sunday, I preached in the largest Baptist Church in the city. The historic building was easily as big and majestic as any European cathedral. I was stunned and humbled to have the opportunity to minister there. I shared a story about two young men; one who was rich, but became poor, and another who was poor, but became rich.

The poor young man lived in poverty and darkness with no apparent way out of his situation. He was a slave of his world. The rich young man and his father had watched this boy struggle for years. Filled with compassion, the father sent his son to rescue the young man out of his misery. The rich son introduced himself to the poor young man.

"My father has given me everything he owns, and I want to give it all to you," he said. "Let me take your misery, and you take my wealth. I will trade my wealth for your poverty."

The poor young man had never experienced such generosity in his whole life and could not understand the great depth of this love.

"Let me do this for you," the rich young man pleaded.

"Poverty owns me and the only way out is death," answered the poor young man.

"I know," the rich man smiled. "But I will pay the price to set you free."

The impoverished young man declared. "I trust you and I accept your invitation."

The poor young man was delivered from his world of poverty to the rich man's home. There he was dressed in fine clothing and his every need was met.

"Friends," I said, "the rich young man's name is Jesus, and the poor young man was me. Jesus is here today with the exact same offer for you. He came to rescue us all out of the poverty of this world, and to offer us a life in His kingdom.

The whole place erupted in a flood of tears. Hundreds gave their lives to Christ Jesus. Where the Spirit of the Lord is, there is liberty. Many found freedom that night.

✠✠✠

Every night during that mission trip I had the same recurring dream.

I was in a large airplane hangar. Thousands of people filled the structure and spilled out onto the tarmac surrounding the building. I stood on a large platform alongside several other pastors.

I spoke to the crowds, sharing the Word of the Lord. People wept, tears flowing down their faces as they surged forward to accept Christ as their savior.

Then I awoke, pondering, "What does it mean?"

I kept that recurring dream to myself until the last day of our trip when I shared it with Dwight.

The last day of our crusade came, and as usual I had no idea where we would be ministering. Dwight and Doru made those arrangements. We just went wherever they told us to go.

The team drove to the edge of town, straight to the airport and onto the tarmac. A huge crowd had already formed outside a large airplane hangar.

It was the place of my recurring dream.

The huge hanger doors and windows were opened wide so the crowd could hear. The seats that were set up inside were filled. Everyone else had to stand for the entire service.

The platform was just as I pictured in the dream. When it came time to deliver my message, I didn't have to give it a second thought. I preached the Word I had already preached multiple times before in my dream.

The results also mirrored my dream in awesome accuracy, as people came to freedom in Christ after a lifetime of bondage. Tears flowed from both the people who came to listen and the people who came to minister.

✠✠✠

Looking back on that mission trip I remember many wonderful events; some humbling and some humorous. Among the greatest results of that trip was the amazing growth that occurred in the local Romanian churches. Most at least doubled in membership; some grew even larger. I returned to the region a few years later to discover a new congregation was meeting in the former KGB training center.

Don't tell me anything is too big for our God to accomplish! A God who can take a small town farm boy and lift him up to minister in places around the world has no problem pulling godless governments to the ground. And just as he is able to direct momentous occasions, he is also interested in guiding every step of our lives along the journey, even the mundane day-to-day steps.

When I was 43, my journey took an unexpected turn. It was at this time that Patti told me she wanted to have another baby. A baby? I had envisioned our future years, and a baby was not in it. Well, it didn't take me long to warm up to the idea, and soon we were in the family way, as they say.

Everything went normally throughout the pregnancy, but the delivery was anything but normal. We had planned a home delivery with midwives assisting. The day came when Patti went into labor. Everything progressed steadily and the time for the baby's birth was near as her water broke.

When the midwife checked her, she discovered an unbroken water sac still intact. She asked to speak with me in the other room. "It could be that there is a double water sac, but there's a slight chance that the baby could be hydrocephalic. If that's the case, we need to leave immediately for the hospital as they both could die."

We quickly loaded the van and off we went, running stop lights and speeding all the way. When we arrived at Vanderbilt Hospital's emergency entrance, a team of specialists were waiting for us. As we opened the van door, Patti had another contraction along with a rush of clear water. She panicked, thinking it was our baby's head, but the midwives were elated as they could tell he was fine.

Benjamin at 15. He not only survived, but thrived.

Our sixth child, Benjamin Hosea, was born right there in the van. Overcome with emotions of relief and great joy we shut the door and went home.

Patti has homeschooled Benjamin all these years and soon he'll be going off to discover what great adventures God has for him. We're so proud to be his parents and I'm so glad I didn't miss out on him!

Chapter 11
Trusting God In All Things

I have been bi-vocational for most of the years that I have served in the ministry. At one point I started my own construction company, and through that company I've met a multitude of believers in unlikely places and been lifted up by their stories of faith. It's been amazing to see how God has orchestrated these seemingly chance meetings to change my world.

While attending a Tuesday morning prayer meeting at Darrell Waltrip's home, I met Terry Anderson, a professional painter (not an artist painter; a house painter). That kind of skill comes in handy when you own a construction company, and Terry shared with me all the secrets of his trade.

"Small world, big kingdom," Terry always said about such divine appointments.

Terry connected me with Doug Steckbeck, who would later become my employee and my best friend. Because of my relationship with Doug, I had the privilege of being his son, Sean's young adult pastor for a season. Sean is truly a man of God, full of the Holy Spirit, who boldly shares the Lord wherever he goes. He and his young family serve the Lord in Israel.

Another so-called chance encounter happened when I met two brothers who invited me to work for their company. It was a family owned Christ-centered kind of business and I fit right in becoming essentially a third brother. I worked for them for a time and then moved on as I felt the Lord's leading. Twenty years later we have reconnected again. I'm now serving as Vice President of the Southeast Region and loving every minute of it.

Nothing is wasted in God's economy. All it takes is our willingness to trust and obey, as the old hymn goes. While that sounds easy, it's not. Sometimes the voice of our flesh deceives us into choosing the wrong path. Wrong paths lead to bondage. The good news of the Gospel is that we can call upon the Lord during our times of trouble, and He will deliver us and set our feet back on the right road again.

Sometimes we confuse our own ideas with God's ideas. I know I've had that experience. Trust me when I say, it is dangerous to confuse the two.

I once had a great idea. I would sell our home, build a larger home in the country, sell that home and use the profits to build a smaller home debt free.

Being debt free is a good thing, so I figured God would approve. Besides, I'd heard of many others who had done this.

"I'm in the home construction business," I thought. "I have an advantage over amateurs who are doing this. This will be a breeze!"

I talked to Patti about it, but she wasn't for the idea. When we drove around the area I thought we should build, all she could do was cry. She loved living in Nolensville and didn't want to leave. Eventually she reluctantly agreed. She would make the sacrifice if we could be debt free in the end. It was a perfect plan I thought. What could go wrong?

Everything, everything could go wrong.

We sold our home, rented and worked on building the new home for a year. It was big. It was beautiful. It was expensive.

We were in so much debt with that house. Not only was the house big, the mortgage payments were big. The utility bills were big. The homeowner's insurance premiums were big. The only thing that wasn't big was my income. It was just enough for us to squeak by, paycheck to paycheck.

We were in bondage to this house.

We lived in that house for three years. We had it up for sale the whole time. No one was interested in buying it.

There's nothing like bondage to make you stop and pray. I finally became desperate and cried out to God.

"I'm sorry, Lord," I began. "I'm in this predicament of my own free will. I made the decision without seeking your will or your blessing. I repent of my self-reliance and ask you to forgive me. I ask you to deliver us out of our trouble. I confess that this is trouble of my own making. I promise to never enter into such a decision again without first asking you. Would you please send someone to buy the house for what I owe on it?"

We sold the house within the week.

God led us to a home we could afford, and after less than a decade we were able to pay off the mortgage. We now own our home free and clear.

We had made a decision when we married we would never own a credit card. We have traveled in many parts of the world and bought homes, cars, and "stuff." We've never paid with a credit card. If we wanted something, we saved our money and paid cash. The only things we ever made payments on were houses and cars. Now we even pay cash for our cars.

Do we drive new cars?

No.

Do we have a large home?

No.

Do we have a nice home?

Yes, we do.

Do we have nice cars?

Yes, we do.

Are they paid for?

You betcha!

It goes against all the wisdom of the world. It takes faith in God to supply all your needs. It requires determination to wait upon His faithfulness. Oh yeah, and it takes a lot of hard work. But there is such peace of mind that comes with being out of debt. There is nothing like it.

Try it. You'll like it.

Chapter 12
Just Walk

One thing our ministry has not been is boring. Over the years we have pastored, preached crusades, taught, led revivals in churches in America and in a number of countries around the world, helped start churches, worked with youth and young adults; whatever was at hand to do we were willing to do.

I've met a number of people who thought ministry is supposed to be glamorous or easy. It's not. Those folks soon become disillusioned and drop out when adversity sets in.

Call us crazy, but we have tried our best to model our life after Jesus. He prayed, and He obeyed. He didn't have a set itinerary. He did what He saw the Father doing, and said what He heard the Father saying.

I've ministered to numerous pastors who were exhausted, burned-out and ready to quit. They thought it was their responsibility to produce tremendous church growth, to build big buildings and lead large staffs. When it didn't work out that way they felt like failures. Once they learned the secret of simply praying and obeying, they became quite successful in life.

There is a common misconception that *it's all up to me*. The truth is, it's not up to you. Your job is to pray and obey. If you are faithful in that, the results are up to God.

Personally, I'd rather live at peace with God and man than to live out my days all torn up inside over some false idea of success.

Besides, you can't get anybody saved anyway. Jesus said, *No one comes to the Father except the Spirit of God draw him*.

It has never been about your education, talent, voice inflection, who you know or what you know. It is all about the anointing of God.

None of my success in life or in the ministry has come as a result of my own efforts. It has all been the result of the working of the Holy Spirit.

I once heard a story about a minister who wanted to impress Billy Graham.

"I go to my office and pray every morning for two hours before I do anything," the minister boasted. "I suppose you must do the same to have the great results you have in ministry.

"No," Graham answered, graciously. "I just talk to the Father all day. Here a little, there a little. He and I are always conversing. That became my way of praying. There have been times when I locked myself away, but mostly I find it easier to just stay connected and not hang up the phone."

I think Jesus modeled this same concept of having fellowship with God, rather than trying to follow some religious formula. Being in constant communication with our Heavenly Father allows us to live in the moment and recognized opportunities as they arise.

The Bible encourages us to be instant in season and out of season. If you know His word and know His voice, you'll be ready at any given time day or night to be used for God's purposes.

I experienced that kind of *in season* usefulness one Sunday after services at The Lord's Chapel. Patti and I started to walk quietly out of the building, being respectful of ministry that was still going on down front, when one of the Elders caught up with us.

"Can you come down front?" he asked. "A woman is asking for you to pray for her."

I didn't know the woman, and I'm not sure how she knew me. Perhaps she had seen me ministering before. All I knew was she needed prayer, and I was happy to pray for her.

Once I got down front the elders let me in the prayer circle. I could tell by her countenance that she was lonely and miserable. I didn't ask her what was wrong. I let the Lord lead my words.

"Who is Sally?" I asked.

The woman's jaw dropped open and her eyes grew wide.

"Sally is my sister," she answered."

"Why do you hate your sister," I asked.

"I do not hate my sister!" she exclaimed, obviously upset.

"Tell me about your sister," I said.

"Sally was born on Father's Day," she stated.

"Stop right there," I said. "The day she was born your dad said, *What a great gift for Father's day*. You hated him for saying that. You believed your father loved Sally more than he loved you. You believed your father thought she was special and you were not. Satan used that to created resentment toward your father and sister throughout your life. That belief has filled you with bitterness and separated you from them. It's made you lonely and bitter, and now it is creating health problems for you."

The woman began to weep.

"You can be healed today," I told her. "All you have to do is forgive them both. Your sister didn't determine the day she was born. It was not her fault. You need to ask the Lord to forgive you, and you need to forgive your sister, although she has never done you any wrong."

The woman prayed for forgiveness and to forgive. In the midst of her tears we could see a change coming over her immediately.

"You must now forgive you father," I continued. "When he declared your sister's birth to be a wonderful Father's Day gift, his comment was not directed to you. He wasn't declaring you to be less important to him. He has always loved you with the same love."

The woman prayed again, to forgive and to be forgiven. You could see deliverance manifesting in her face.

Once more I addressed her.

"You need to forgive your heavenly Father," I said. "He had control over the day of your sister's birth. He chose it in His wisdom for His own purpose. You must trust Him. There is a reason your sister was born on Father's Day. Forgive Him and ask Him to forgive you."

With this final prayer her countenance turned to radiance and the peace of God washed over her. She was set free from the bondage of bitterness and loneliness. I knew she was going to go make things right with her sister, and although her earthly father had already died, I knew her Heavenly Father would extend that grace.

Of course God has never sinned and does not need our forgiveness. But our bitterness can be bound up by unforgiveness when we blame God for situations in our lives. When we exercise forgiveness, God moves to remove the bitterness.

Had I prepared for that day?

Yes. I knew the Word from study, and I knew the Father's voice from our long relationship. I was available for His use at that moment in time; not because I was a preacher, or an evangelist, but because I was a believer.

Signs and wonders follow those who believe. If you are a believer, you are a candidate for being used by His Holy Spirit at any given moment.

✠✠✠

My boys played baseball when they were young. It's not a violent sport, but that doesn't mean it is without risk. On one occasion a player got hit in the nose by a ball. His nose was bleeding profusely and a crowd started around the boy. I reached through the crowd, laid my hand on the top of his head and quickly prayed over him:

According to Ezekiel 16:6, I see you in your blood and I command the bleeding to stop in the name of Jesus.

The bleeding stopped immediately. Before anyone could look around, my boys and I walked away. No one saw who had done this thing, and I certainly took no credit for it. It was just another day in the life of an ordinary believer.

A few days later while standing in line waiting to check out at the neighborhood grocery store, I chanced to overhear a conversation. The clerk behind the counter was telling the lady checking out about a miracle.

"Did you hear what happened at the ball field the other night?" she asked. "A boy got hit in the face with a baseball and had a serious nose bleed. Someone commanded his nose to stop bleeding in the name of Isaiah, and just like that the bleeding stopped."

"No," I interrupted. "He was quoting Ezekiel 16:6 not Isaiah." I proceeded to tell them what the verse said.

I didn't tell them 'that guy' was me. After all, I wasn't the one who stopped the bleeding. It wasn't about me. It was about God getting the glory for what He did. This was just an example of how God watches over His Word to perform it.

Chapter 13
Time Flies

It is amazing. One day you're 24 years old, ministering on the streets of Chicago with your young bride. You blink, and you're 61 years old with five children, their spouses and ten grandchildren. Time truly does fly. In the words of King David, *A man's life is like a mere breath; His days are like a passing shadow.*

The events I've recounted in these pages are but a few of the highlights of my life. Much has been left out. My purpose has not been to glorify myself, or point out the miracles or signs and say, 'Look at me!'

The point I want to make is that I've lived what I believe to be a normal Christian life. I hope my story encourages you to walk by faith in Him, day by day, making room for Him to orchestrate divine appointments.

There was a popular teaching a few years back that encouraged people to *go out and find your destiny in God.* I always thought that a strange teaching. It implies that I am somehow in charge of where I go in God's kingdom.

I believe if you love God with all your heart, study His Word so you know the difference between right and wrong, and walk with Him daily so you know His voice when you hear it, wherever He leads you is your destiny.

If you try to do it yourself, in your own power and ability, you'll end up with a false destiny. But you are not called to please other people or yourself. You are called to please the One you serve.

You can try to make your own destiny. You can ask Him to bless your thing, to ride along with you as you travel your own path. He promised to never leave you nor forsake you, but if you are traveling your own path, He'll let you take the consequences of your choices.

I much prefer the lifestyle described by the Word: *He who is holy, who is true, who has the key of David, opens doors and no one will shut them; and shuts doors that no one can open.* The walk I have chosen has been to listen and to obey.

Have I always listened well?

No, but I have seen His hand at work in everything even correcting the road map of my life.

One of my favorite Bible verses is Psalm 34:19:

Many are the afflictions of the righteous: but the Lord delivers him out of them all.

I've certainly found that to be true in my life. I sought the Lord, and He heard me and delivered me out of all my troubles. He is my salvation and there is salvation in no other name. Our God is God. If God is for us, who can be against us.

These are truths that I have hidden in my heart that I might not sin against God.

You might think sinning against God means doing bad things. But the Greek word for sin literally means *to miss the mark*. Instead of thinking about sin in terms of degrees of good and evil, it's really about taking the right or the wrong road. If you say you're following Christ and His word, but have chosen a path that God did not choose for you, you have missed the mark.

Since He is the Author and Finisher of our faith, doesn't it make sense to trust Him in all things relating to our life?

He is the way, the truth and the life. Choosing a different path, one that is not supported by His word, won't lead to life, but to death. It might not lead to immediate physical death, although that too is possible, but it will certainly lead to suffering.

Consider a simple game of darts as an example of how this works. If I keep my eye on the target and throw straight and true, I'll hit the board and get a good score. If I get distracted and look away as I'm throwing a dart, I might miss the board completely. Not only will I fail to score any points, I've put a hole in the wall that now has to be repaired.

Of course the wages of sin is far worse than making a tiny hole in the drywall. The wages of sin is death. And sin doesn't just affect you. It also causes suffering in the lives of others; those close to you and potentially to people you don't even know.

Anger, jealousy, pride, lust, envy and a host of other factors can distract our minds and cause us to take our eyes off Christ. That's why the Word encourages us to examine ourselves to ensure our attitudes, desires and relationships are on course.

Ultimately missing the mark is all about selfishness. We take our eyes off of Christ and seek our own path. Christ laid down His life for others and calls us to be willing to do the same.

If we walk in the light of His word it is easy to examine ourselves. Without His Spirit and truth it is impossible. It is our nature to choose our own comfort over another's.

It is work to be Christ-like, but the inevitable result is life, and life more abundant. Just as it is better to give than to receive, it is better to obey than to sacrifice.

Sometimes we put our eyes on the sacrifice as if it is a good thing. A sacrifice is a loss. We offer a sacrifice as a result of disobedience. Isn't it much better to obey so no sacrifice is required?

Adults tend to be wiser than their children, in part because they have already made all the common mistakes and learned from them. They have suffered from bad choices, and don't want their kids to suffer the same fate.

The wages of sin is death. Praise God, we don't have to suffer death, separation from peace, and joy. Jesus already paid the price for our disobedience. And He sent the Holy Spirit to comfort, guide and counsel those of us who come after Him.

The Holy Spirit has encouraged me in good times, comforted me in sorrow and delivered me out of all my troubles. If you ask Him to come into your life, to fill you and to give purpose to your life, He will do the same for you.

Why am I talking about these things instead of testifying about other miracles I've seen? Because I want to encourage you to fully trust in the Lord.

Before miracles can happen, the atmosphere must be conducive for the Spirit of God to move. Remember Simon, the magician who offered to pay money for the ability to perform miracles? His heart was wrong and the Apostle Peter rebuked him for thinking he could buy the gifts of God.

If your heart towards God is pure, and your faith is sure, these signs will follow you as they have followed me and many others I know.

I am nobody special, but I am convinced in whom I believe. He is my all in all. I trust Him. Yes, I still miss the mark. But He remains faithful to guide me back to center, and He continues performing the miraculous around me; not for my glory, but for His.

Living life this way hasn't always been fun, but it's never been dull. It has been an awesome privilege to participate in God's workings. The great thing is, such a privilege is not limited to a chosen few. You too can be used mightily of God. I hope you will find out just how great His love toward you is, and see His mighty hand at work in your life.

He is the same yesterday, today and forever.

Bonus

Here is one last example of a miracle of a different kind to show how God has already thought your life out and made interchanges along the way.

We were on a mission trip in Jamaica, holding meetings in the small village churches. While I was preaching a man wandered in and sat down with our team. When I gave the altar call he came forward. He spoke in broken English, but we managed to communicate the Gospel and that night he gave his heart back to Christ.

"What brought you here during the middle of the service?" I asked him.

"I was next door at the bar and I heard your voice," the man replied. "I recognized it from 15 years ago when I was only a boy. I knew I had to get to you."

"I wasn't in Jamaica 15 years ago," I replied.

"No," the man explained. "Fifteen years ago you preached in my father's church in Romania. I accepted Christ then, but I have gone away from the Lord. I'm here in Jamaica working on a construction project trying to make money for my family. When I heard your voice, I knew God brought you here and I had to come back to Christ. So here I am."

It just goes to show you how much God loves you. You may be in some remote place and think He's forgotten about you or doesn't love you anymore because of the mess you've made, but that's a lie. The Father is always looking for you to come home to Him. He's always waiting with the light on.

If God had a refrigerator, your picture would be on it!

✠✠✠

One evening a friend's wife called me. "I think my husband is having a heart attack," she cried, "and he refuses to go to the hospital. He insists you come here and pray for him."

I went right over to their house. I had shared the Lord with this man for years, telling him he needed to give his heart to Jesus. He was always too busy and wanted to put it off until later. He owned a business that consumed him, the Lord showed me the stress of it was weighing heavy upon him.

"You are having a melt down," I told him once I arrived. "You need Christ in your life or the stress is going to kill you."

I started telling stories I thought might build up his faith. I went on and on, until he gripped his chest and just looked at me with pleading eyes. I suddenly realized he didn't need my stories. He was already ready to receive Christ.

"I think you want me to stop talking and lead you in the prayer to receive Christ," I said.

"Please!" he said.

The peace that passes understanding came upon him as soon as we prayed, and his pain went away. Several years have come and gone since that day, and he has never suffered a heart attack. The peace of Christ in his life has curbed the stress.

I said all that to say, after all these stories, you may be where he was. Perhaps you just want me to stop talking and lead you in a prayer to receive Christ as your Lord and Savior. Pray this prayer:

Jesus I believe you are the one and only true Son of God. I believe that you went to the cross and died to pay the price for my sins, and that God your Father raised you from the dead. I accept that you have life and it more abundantly for me as my Lord and Savior. I ask you to come into my heart, purge me of sin and make me a new creature. Take my life and make it what you have always intended it to be. Amen.

Welcome to the family and the peace that passes all understanding, through Christ Jesus. He is the same yesterday, today and forever.

Amen.

About The Author

Don McCain is simply a believer who has served as a messenger of the Lord to many countries for more than 40 years. He has operated in all of the five-fold ministry gifts as the Lord required. As an apostle he helped start churches. As a prophet he provided spiritual direction to groups of believers. As a pastor he cared for congregations and as a teacher he has led small business groups and conferences.

Today Don serves as Vice President of sales for a growing company. In this capacity he daily proves that the truths shared from the pulpit all these years, work for all believers and not just those in full time ministry. He leads others in understanding these truths and becoming successful because of them.

Don's wife labeled him, 'The Bridge Man,' a person used of the Lord to help others in life transitions – here a word, there a word, line upon line and precept upon precept in the making of Disciples.

He is the founder of *Hearts For Souls Ministry* and Director of "My God is God"campaign, now known as the "There is Hope" campaign.

Made in the USA
Charleston, SC
24 May 2014